T0345607

# THE HITTITES

LOST CIVILIZATIONS

The books in this series explore the rise and fall of the great civilizations and peoples of the ancient world. Each book considers not only their history but their art, culture and lasting legacy and asks why they remain important and relevant in our world today.

*Already published:*

*The Aztecs*  Frances F. Berdan
*The Barbarians*  Peter Bogucki
*Egypt*  Christina Riggs
*The Etruscans*  Lucy Shipley
*The Goths*  David M. Gwynn
*The Greeks*  Philip Matyszak
*The Hittites*  Damien Stone
*The Inca*  Kevin Lane
*The Indus*  Andrew Robinson
*The Maya*  Megan E. O'Neil
*Nubia*  Sarah M. Schellinger
*The Persians*  Geoffrey Parker and Brenda Parker
*The Phoenicians*  Vadim S. Jigoulov
*The Sumerians*  Paul Collins

# THE
# HITTITES
## LOST CIVILIZATIONS

DAMIEN STONE

REAKTION BOOKS

Published by Reaktion Books Ltd
Unit 32, Waterside
44–48 Wharf Road
London N1 7UX, UK
www.reaktionbooks.co.uk

First published 2023
Copyright © Damien Stone 2023

Printed and bound in India by Replika Press Pvt. Ltd

A catalogue record for this book is available from the British Library

ISBN  978 1 78914 684 4

# CONTENTS

# CHRONOLOGY

| | |
|---|---|
| *c.* 9600–8000 BC | Circular groups of carved T-shaped pillars are constructed at Göbekli Tepe (some of the earliest known man-made structures). The site has been dubbed 'the world's oldest temple' |
| *c.* 7400–5200 BC | Occupation of settlement at Çatalhöyük – one of the earliest villages in the world |
| *c.* 3500–3000 BC | Writing is invented in Mesopotamia by the Sumerians. The cuneiform script would later be adopted by the Hittites |
| *c.* 2500 BC | Great Sphinx of Giza is constructed for Khafre. Representing Egyptian kings in this form subsequently became a pharaonic tradition. The mythical creature was adopted in the imagery of many other cultures of the ancient Near East and Mediterranean, including the Hittites |
| *c.* 2334–2154 BC | The period of the world's first empire, the Akkadians, founded by King Sargon the Great. Documents from his reign attest to the earliest mention of the Hattians in Anatolia. The language of the Akkadians remained in use by the peoples of Mesopotamia until around the start of the sixth |

|  |  |
|---|---|
|  | century BC. Akkadian became the language of international diplomacy, used for communication between major powers, including the Hittites |
| *c.* 21st–18th century BC | Merchants from Assyria operate trading colonies in Anatolia known as *kārū*. The most notable of these was at Kültepe |
| *c.* 18th century BC | The exploits of Pithana and his son Anitta are documented in the first known text composed in the Hittite language |
| *c.* 1800 BC | Earliest-known Old Babylonian version of the *Epic of Gilgamesh*, a myth that enjoyed popularity throughout the ancient Near East |
| *c.* 1650 BC | The founding of the Hittite Old Kingdom. Hattusa becomes the Hittite capital under King Hattusili I |
| *c.* 1595 BC | The Hittite king Mursili I sacks the city of Babylon, bringing an end to the Old Babylonian empire |
| *c.* 1400 BC | Beginning of the Hittite New Kingdom |
| *c.* 1360–1332 BC | The Amarna letters attest an age of international diplomacy between the powers of the ancient Near East |
| *c.* 1350–1322 BC | The kingdom becomes an empire during the reign of Suppiluliuma I, regarded as the greatest of the Hittite kings |
| 1274 BC | The Battle of Qadesh takes place between the Egyptians (under Ramesses II) and the Hittite |

Empire (ruled by Muwatalli II). It results in a stalemate, leading to the drawing up of the Egyptian–Hittite peace treaty some fifteen years later

c. 1250 BC — Traditional date for the Trojan War, as given by Herodotus

c. 1180 BC — Destruction of Hattusa and the collapse of the Hittite Empire. Several other states also disappeared around this time, in what has become known as the Bronze Age collapse

c. 1180–700 BC — Traces of Hittite culture and the Luwian writing system continue being used by the Neo-Hittite (or Syro-Hittite) states

8th century BC — Height of the Phrygian state in Anatolia, based at their capital of Gordion. There is a level of Phrygian occupation at Hattusa, some five hundred years after the Hittite evacuation of the site

c. 730–700 BC — Hesiod composes the *Theogony*, which describes the origins of the ancient Greek gods. There are remarkable similarities between this work and the much earlier Hurrio-Hittite Kumarbi cycle. Traders were likely responsible for not only exchanging goods between east and west, but the sharing of such stories orally

546 BC — Cyrus the Great conquers the Lydian king Croesus, bringing Asia Minor under Persian rule. The Lydians are credited with the invention of coinage

| | |
|---|---|
| 499–449 BC | The Graeco-Persian wars. A memorable episode in Herodotus' *Histories* describes Xerxes' attempt to cross from Asia into Europe by building pontoon bridges across the Hellespont (the modern Dardanelles). A storm destroyed the structure before the army was able to cross. The enraged Persian king was reported to have punished the Hellespont with three hundred whiplashes, throwing fetters into the water and branding it with red-hot irons |
| *c.* 350 BC | The Mausoleum at Halicarnassus, one of the Seven Wonders of the Ancient World, is built (at what is now Bodrum on the west coast of Turkey) |
| 323 BC | After forging a huge empire, which stretched from Greece to India, Alexander the Great dies in Babylon |
| 282–133 BC | The Hellenistic Attalid dynasty governs the kingdom of Pergamon in Asia Minor. The fall of the state to the Roman Republic sees many Greek cities in Turkey (such as Ephesus) become Roman. |
| 27 BC | The Roman Republic becomes the Roman Empire under Augustus Caesar |
| *c.* AD 5 | Birth of St Paul the Apostle. Born to a Jewish family from Tarsus, he converted to Christianity after being struck by a vision of the Ascension of Jesus, which left him blinded for three days. Over the sixty years of his life, he travelled extensively, preaching and establishing a number of Christian communities in Turkey |

| | |
|---|---|
| 330 | The beginnings of the Byzantine Empire, marked by the emperor Constantine founding a second Rome on the site of Byzantium. It was named after him, as Constantinople. Much later, it would become Istanbul |
| 527–65 | The reign of Emperor Justinian I, who was responsible for a flourishing of Byzantine culture, including the construction of the Hagia Sophia. Both he and his wife, the empress Theodora, are saints in the Eastern Orthodox church and share a feast day on 14 November |
| 570–632 | Life of the prophet Muhammad, founder of the Islamic faith |
| 10th century | After an absence of more than two millennia following the Bronze Age collapse, the double-headed eagle re-emerges as a motif in art and heraldry of the Byzantine Empire. Did they perhaps stumble upon the thirteenth-century BC Hittite renditions of this icon, such as that at Yazılıkaya? |
| 1326 | Osman I, the founding father of the Ottomans, takes the city of Bursa |
| 1453 | Mehmed II conquers the city of Constantinople and makes it the new Ottoman capital, bringing an end to the Byzantine Empire. Instead of destroying the Hagia Sophia, he converts it into a mosque. The Christian icons upon its walls were plastered over, essentially preserving them for modern discovery. |

| | |
|---|---|
| 1520–66 | Reign of Suleiman the Magnificent. A golden age for the Ottoman Empire |
| 1834 | The ruins of Hattusa are discovered by the French explorer Charles Texier |
| 1844 | The Ottomans adopt the motif of a white crescent and star on a red background as their flag. Known as *al bayrak*, it remains the national flag of the Turkish Republic today |
| 1880 | Archibald Henry Sayce identifies the Bronze Age people of central Anatolia as the Hittites of the Bible. Although Sayce made some fundamental errors in his identification, the attribution remains |
| 1914–18 | Allied with Germany, the Ottomans fight in the First World War. The Allied powers attempt to take Constantinople via the Gallipoli peninsula, but after eight months of fighting at the cove, they are forced to withdraw the invasion force. The Gallipoli campaign thus became regarded as a great Ottoman victory. It saw the future Turkish president Kemal Atatürk rise to prominence as a commander. The heroic spirit of the Australian and New Zealander (ANZAC) troops on the opposing side at Gallipoli is memorialized in both these countries on 25 April. The Ottoman Empire was ultimately defeated and the First World War greatly reduced its territory |
| 1923 | Following the decline of the Ottoman Empire, the Republic of Turkey is established. Ankara becomes the capital |

| 1934 | Mustafa Kemal Pasha adopts the name of Atatürk, designating him as 'the Father of Turks' |
|------|------|
| 1970 | The Turkish government give a replica of the Egyptian–Hittite peace treaty to the United Nations. A facsimile of the cuneiform document is hung outside the Security Council Chamber |
| 1978 | Sculptor Nusret Suman creates the Hittite Sun Course Monument in Ankara's Sıhhiye Square, modelled off the Hattian bronze standards from Alaca Höyük |
| 2007 | An email from an anonymous art collective is circulated in Ankara, on the eve of the Turkish general election, entitled 'Hitit Güneşi Ankara'ya Yeniden Doğuyor' ('The Hittite Sun is Rising Once Again'). The group protest against the change of Ankara's city logo. They call for reinstating the pre-Hittite sun disc, which had been replaced by the emblem of a mosque as the official symbol of the Turkish capital. A reflection that the Hittites have become a source of national pride and symbolic of secular Turkish identity |
| 2021 | Over four hundred Indo-European languages are spoken today by 46 per cent of the world's population (3.2 billion). This language family includes English. The earliest surviving written language of the Indo-European family is Hittite |

Amulet of a Hittite god, 13th–13th century BCE, silver. He wears a kilt and the conical crown associated with divinity. The figure's arm is raised in a smiting position, suggesting this may be a representation of the thundering Storm-god.

# PROLOGUE

The seventeenth century BC saw a dynasty of kings emerge speaking an Indo-European language in what is now central Turkey. Their culture was a quirky combination of established ancient Near Eastern practices blended with native Anatolian customs. As their empire expanded, until its fall at the start of the twelfth century BC, it continued to absorb traditions from conquered peoples. Recognized for their military prowess among the contemporary civilizations of the Bronze Age, they are now known as the Hittites. This book aims to give an overview of the Hittites and their customs, in the hope of increasing the recognition and renown that these often-overlooked ancient people deserve.

The term 'Anatolia' is commonly used as the name for the homeland of the Hittites, the highland plateau region of modern Turkey. It is of Greek origin, first used much later (in the tenth century AD), deriving from *anatole* meaning 'rising'– as the Greeks looked east, it was from Anatolia that the Sun rose. The Hittites themselves referred to their homeland simply as the land of Hatti. This designation is not to be confused with the Hattians, forerunners in the region prior to the arrival of the Hittites – several unique cultures had already developed in this area prior to the emergence of the Hittite society. Likewise, the Hittites would not be the last – from the Phrygians and Graeco-Romans to the Seljuks and Ottomans, this area would remain prime real estate.

The high-altitude Anatolian plateau where Hittites dwelled faced climatic extremes, alternating hot, dry summers and cold, snowy winters. Surrounded by mountains, during the Bronze Age this semi-arid area was thickly forested. The Pontic mountain range lies to the north of the plateau, while the Taurus Mountains border the south. To the west lies a fertile river valley. Rivers give rise to great civilizations, and for the Hittites theirs was the Maraššantiya. In the classical era it was called the Halys River, and today it is known by the modern Turkish name of the Kızılırmak (Red River). However, it was rainfall rather than irrigation that offered the main supply of water in this region, on which the Hittite agrarian-based economy depended. Springs also played an important role as a water source for the Hittites, the capital of Hattusa being supplied by seven springs. The borders of the Hittite state were constantly shifting but reached their furthest extent at the end of the fourteenth century BC. Territory outside of the Hittite homeland in central Anatolia was controlled not directly but through vassalage. The Hittites were not a seafaring people, as their central homeland was landlocked. On the seldom occasion that they engaged in naval enterprises, they relied on the ships of their allies or vassal states.

Hittite society was divided into three main spheres: the religious, the agricultural and the martial. At the head of society was the Hittite king, who oversaw the success of each sphere. All depended on a monarch's ability to maintain order, particularly by preserving relations with the heavenly gods. Offending the gods could result in plague, famine, invasion, military failure and civil strife, all of which were regarded as forms of divine retribution. A team of his most trusted officials assisted the king in maintaining this balance, which kept society operating. The two major sources of economic revenue were agriculture and the booty (as well as the subsequent tribute) brought back from subjugating neighbouring states. The vast majority of people lived outside cities in farming villages. Further archaeological work and study remains to be done to comprehend the experience of these lower classes. Our understanding of Hittite society is still highly skewed towards the exploits of royalty, whose bureaucracy produced the majority of Hittite texts. Nonetheless, these documents are rich resources, and I have quoted from them extensively throughout

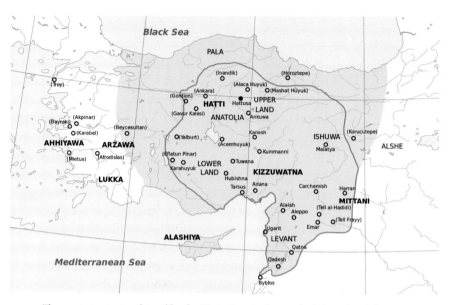

The greatest extents achieved by the Hittite Empire (green shaded area) and the territory it held in circa 1350–1300 BC (dark green line).

this book, allowing those ancient voices to speak to the modern reader.

Hittite history is marked by two periods of influence. Using the Middle Chronology for dating the ancient Near East, the Hittite Old Kingdom refers to the era from the mid-seventeenth century BC to the end of the fifteenth century BC. The Hittite New Kingdom began with the reign of King Tudhaliya I/II in circa 1400 BC and concluded with the collapse of the empire around 1200 BC. But before we journey back to the Bronze Age, we must begin our exploration with some more recent events, as two hundred years ago, the Hittites were largely unknown beyond the scattered references to people by this name in the Bible.

## ONE

# REDISCOVERING A LOST CIVILIZATION

Unlike the ancient Greeks and Romans, who were never really forgotten and whose histories were transmitted to us by the copyists of the medieval period, the fall of Hittite civilization obscured the memory of this warrior culture for more than 3,000 years. In AD 1834, its story began to re-emerge. That year had brought a French explorer, Charles Texier, to Anatolia in search of the remains of the Roman settlement Tavium. Surveying archaeological ruins in the modern locale of Boğazköy, he quickly realized that what he had found was much older. The foundations of walls belonging to a great city were visible. Its monumental gates were carved with strange stone figures – lions, sphinxes and a bare-chested warrior. Near the remains of the city, Texier explored a rocky outcrop that the Turkish locals call Yazılıkaya (Inscribed Rock). It was carved with many more unusual figures in relief and an unknown hieroglyphic script. Texier was fascinated by what he saw and made sketches of his mysterious findings. Though he did not know it, Texier was in the capital of one of the great Bronze Age empires: the city of Hattusa. It would be some time before it was identified as such. In 1839 Texier encountered a relief carved into a rocky pass located some 20 kilometres (12½ mi.) from Izmir. Following his lead, the archaeologist Karl Richard Lepsius made a trip to this site, known as the Karabel relief, in 1840. The sculpture depicts a warrior figure in profile wearing a conical hat and shoes with upward-curled toes. He holds both a bow and a spear. The relief had actually been described in the fifth century BC by the ancient Greek historian

Charles Texier's illustration of the central scene of Chamber A at Yazılıkaya.

Herodotus, who misidentified it as a depiction of an Egyptian pharaoh. Despite no resemblance to Egyptian art, Texier and Lepsius willingly accepted this false attribution. This view was quickly disproven, and its likeness to the rock reliefs at Yazılıkaya was noted. When the hieroglyphic script accompanying the carving was translated much later, the figure was identified as Tarkasnawa, a thirteenth-century BC king of Mira, a Hittite vassal state.[1] Stones featuring this same hieroglyphic script had also begun turning up in Syria in the nineteenth century. Travellers noted that blocks of stone inscribed with the strange hieroglyphs had been repurposed in the construction of buildings around the Bazaar of Hama and even built into the wall of a mosque in Aleppo. Against the protestations of locals, who believed they had healing powers, the hieroglyphic stones were pulled out in 1872 and transported to Constantinople to be studied.

In 1880 the mysterious civilization was given a name. At a symposium of the Society of Biblical Archaeology, Reverend Archibald Henry Sayce identified the creators of the hieroglyphic script and builders of the city discovered by Texier as the Hittites (or 'Sons of Heth') of the Bible. Famously, in the Old Testament, David lusts after Bathsheba, the wife of a Hittite named Uriah. David thus arranges for the death of the Hittite warrior: 'Place Uriah in the

The Karabel relief, 13th century BC. The relief depicts Tarkasnawa, king of the Hittite vassal state of Mira. On viewing this relief in the 5th century BC Herodotus misidentified the figure as that of the Egyptian king Sesostris.

Bilingual silver seal. The text identifies the owner in both cuneiform and Luwian hieroglyph as Tarkasnawa, king of Mira.

front line of the fiercest battle and withdraw from him, so that he may be struck down and die' (2 Samuel 11:15). He is killed, allowing Bathsheba to remarry the Hebrew king, after a period of mourning. Another passage equates the military might of the Hittites with that of the Egyptians, as the Arameans exclaim, 'Look, the king of Israel has hired the Hittite and Egyptian kings to attack us' (2 Kings 7:6). There were many errors in Sayce's arguments, which placed the Hittites administrative centre in Syria and dated the empire to the Iron Age.[2] William Wright's publication *The Empire of the Hittites* followed in 1884 – the first attempt at a study of their civilization. Whether the Hittites of the Bible share an identity with the civilization based around Hattusa is still debated. For one thing, the Hittites of central Anatolia never referred to themselves as 'Hittites'. They referred to their land as Hatti and their language, Nesite. Egyptian documents call them the 'kingdom of Kheta'. The name Hittite is still used today for describing the Anatolian Bronze Age empire simply as a matter of convention.

Late in the nineteenth century, the German engineer and archaeologist Karl Humann took casts of the reliefs at Yazılıkaya (they can still be seen in Berlin's Vorderasiatisches Museum). This was during an expedition in Asia Minor, which saw Humann involved in the excavation of the ancient Greek city of Pergamon. It was he who uncovered the famed Pergamon Altar and oversaw its transportation back to Germany. German archaeologists came to dominate excavation in the region, under the patronage of the German Oriental Society (Deutsche Orient-Gesellschaft).

## An important digression: Hittite language(s) and decipherment

Excavations were begun at Hattusa in 1893–4 by the French archaeologist Ernest Chantre and were continued in 1906 under the direction of the German Hugo Winckler. Accompanied by his Turkish–Greek colleague, Theodor Makridi, Winckler's excavations yielded a large quantity of written documents on clay tablets. They were composed in cuneiform script. Cuneiform (of Latin origin, meaning 'wedge-shaped') characters were created from combinations of vertical, horizontal and diagonal wedges impressed by a reed stylus in wet clay. The script was used to render several different languages spoken in the Hittite Empire. At the time of the first archaeological excavations at Hattusa, one of these was already known and had been translated. This was the Akkadian cuneiform. Winckler was able to read these tablets, as this language had already been deciphered in the first half of the nineteenth century. Akkadian was the successor to Sumerian, the world's first known written language for which cuneiform had been invented. The conquest of Mesopotamia by the Akkadian Empire in the third millennium BC saw the Akkadians adopt the Sumerian script to render their own Semitic language. Other civilizations, in turn, adopted cuneiform to document their languages, though Akkadian remained the lingua franca for much of the ancient Near East. Dialects of Akkadian were spoken by the Babylonians and Assyrians. The Amarna archive, a cache of diplomatic cuneiform letters between kings, was discovered in Egypt in 1887. The majority of the letters were written in Akkadian cuneiform. They document the correspondence between the international powers of the fourteenth century BC, including the Hittites. The Akkadian documents at Hattusa reflect Akkadian's importance as an international language during the Hittite period.

Other tablets being unearthed were written in cuneiform script but in a completely unknown language. Though the cuneiform symbols could be read, they made no sense. This was the main language of the Hittites. Hittite (originally known as Nesite) is the earliest known Indo-European language. The modern Romance languages and Germanic languages (including English) belong to this same family. This relationship is evident in the Hittite word for 'water', which is simply *watar*. The Czech linguist Bedřich Hrozný recognized this when he made the breakthrough of deciphering a sentence of Hittite language during the First World War: *nu* NINDA-*an ezzatteni watar-ma ekutteni*. Rather poetically, this statement concerns the most basic acts of human consumption: 'You will eat bread and drink water.'[3] Hrozný deduced that the Hittite word *ezzatteni* was the verb 'to eat', due to its resemblance to the modern German *essen*. Parallels were found with other languages, and Hrozný published his findings in a 1915 article entitled 'The Solution to the Hittite Problem'. This was followed by a book on Hittite grammar in 1917. It is thanks to this breakthrough that Hrozný is regarded as the father of Hittitology.

Like other cuneiform languages, Hittite uses three types of characters. *Syllabograms* are phonetic characters that represent syllables. *Logograms* (characters representing whole words) were directly imported from Sumerian and Akkadian. The symbol NINDA in the breakthrough sentence, for instance, is the Sumerian logogram for bread. *Determinatives* are not pronounced but used to classify nouns that comes after – such as the star-shaped DINGAR, which occurs before the name of a deity, or LUGAL, which identifies the name of a king. Some surviving texts are bilingual, featuring the same document or a vocabulary list in multiple languages. In addition to Hittite and Akkadian, several other cuneiform languages have been found at Hattusa. The most notable was the language of the Hurrians, a people who were both a regular military threat (until Suppiluliuma 1's conquest of the Mittanian Empire) as well as hugely influential on Hittite culture.

As opposed to a condensed and relatively easy-to-master alphabetic script, cuneiform languages, such as Hittite, have hundreds of characters and take years to learn. Thus the majority of people living in Hittite society were illiterate. Only those involved in the bureaucracy of elite society (as well as a few ritual practitioners who authored the instructions for various rites) required the skill. Scribes formed an important part of the workforce. These individuals were taught the writing system in scribal schools – an education largely based on the repetitive task of copying texts. The tablets they penned have shaped our understanding of Hittite society, from the documenting of local legal rulings to the drafting of treaties between international powers. Some of the scribes who trained in the capital would have been deployed to other administrative centres, to allow for the flow of information across the empire. Occasionally, official correspondence penned by scribes included a brief informal letter at the end of the document. These notes check in on how an affiliate scribe at the receiving end might be faring. A scribe stationed abroad might request his counterpart back in Hattusa to report on the state of his assets or family. In one such exchange, a certain Uzzu complains that the maid he has been sent by his fellow scribe was stealing household valuables.[4] These marginalia provide a rather personal touch to our history of the Hittites, which is otherwise largely dominated by kings.

One script used by the Hittites baffled modern scholars for some time. These were the enigmatic hieroglyphs used in rock carvings such as those found above the Karabel relief and at Yazılıkaya. While some logograms of the script were identified in the 1930s, the major breakthrough towards its decipherment was in 1946 with the discovery of a bilingual text at Karatepe. The Azatiwada inscription is written in both this hieroglyphic script and Phoenician. This stone slab boasts the exploits of a Neo-Hittite king from the eighth century BC. Azatiwada describes himself as being blessed by the Sun. True to the style of a Near Eastern king, he describes the utopia he has brought to his people: 'In my days I extended the borders of Adanawa, on the one hand towards the west and on the other hand towards the east. And in those places which were formerly feared, where a man feared to walk the road, in my days even women walked with spindles.'[5]

The writing system has become known as Luwian or Anatolian hieroglyphs, as it rendered the Luwian language.[6] This language is a close relative of Hittite, spoken by the Hatti's neighbours to the south and west. The Luwians fell under the control of the Hittites

Luwian hieroglyphs carved upon the Südburg structure at Hattusa.

and these two civilizations came to share many cultural traditions. In the late period of the empire the Hittites used Luwian hieroglyphs for royal seals and in monumental inscriptions. The reason why the Hittites started using this second script is unclear. One persuasive argument maintains that hieroglyphs were implemented for reasons of identity. Competition with Egypt and Mesopotamia led to the adoption of a writing system unique to the Hittite homeland.[7] Luwian hieroglyphic script continued being used in Anatolia after the fall of the Hittite Empire by its cultural successors, the Neo-Hittites.

## Excavations

As noted, Winckler's early excavations at Hattusa focused on uncovering tablets. Some 30,000 tablets or tablet fragments have been unearthed from Hattusa, including the notable Egyptian–Hittite peace treaty. However, the excavation techniques utilized to do so were problematic. Winckler left no notes on the location of his finds – thus we do not know about the organization of the documents or their relationship to each other. Some of the tablets were damaged during excavation, while others were deemed to be too fragmentary and were dumped. Winckler excavated at the site until 1912. Passing away the following year, he did not live to see the decryption of the Hittite language on all of those tablets that he had excavated. The first interest in the mapping of Hattusa and the excavation of its buildings was by Otto Puchstein, who joined Winckler at the site in 1907; Kurt Bittel was the first to record stratigraphy at the site in the 1930s. The Second World War brought excavations to a halt at the end of the decade. Excavations resumed in 1952, with Bittel returning as site director. He remained in the position until 1977. He has since been followed by Peter Neve (1978–93), Jürgen Seeher (1994–2005) and Andreas Schachner (2006–present).

Other archaeological excavations have also been instrumental in advancing our knowledge of Hittite society. Cuneiform archives found at several other sites have facilitated their identification as Hittite regional centres within the ancient homeland. Maşat Höyük was first excavated in the 1970s and has been identified as the ancient settlement of Tapikka. The site of Ortaköy was identified in 1989 as Sapinuwa, an administrative and religious centre that also functioned as a military base and, occasionally, a royal residence of Hittite kings. Excavations at modern Kuşaklı, beginning in 1992, have established the site as ancient Sarissa, a religious centre. Other archaeological sites with a Hittite presence await identification. Alaca Höyük clearly played an important role in the Hittite Empire, given its notable sculptural programme, but it lacks any inscription that identifies its ancient name (although several have been hypothesized). There are many other places, such as Tarhuntassa, that, although they played key roles in Hittite history, have eluded modern discovery. The story of the Hittites is far from complete. Texts and other new findings continue to be published and interpreted, furthering our understanding of this rich Anatolian culture.

# TWO

# POLITICAL AND
# MILITARY HISTORY

U nlike other civilizations of the ancient Near East, no king lists survive for the rulers of the Hittites. We have only a handful of absolute dates, based on other civilizations' documentation of events (the most notable example being the Battle of Qadesh fought with Egypt in 1274 BC). Therefore, dates assigned to the reigns of Hittite kings are approximate and vary between different scholarly studies. It is uncertain, for example, exactly how many kings had the name Tudhaliya. As such, the figure of Tudhaliya I is sometimes referred to as Tudhaliya II or even Tudhaliya I/II.

### Origins: Hattians and the old Assyrian trading colonies

The Hittites were not the first society to develop in ancient Turkey. For thousands of years prior to their emergence, many fascinating peoples dwelled there. Some of the Anatolian ideas we first encounter at these early sites persisted into the Hittite period. Notable is the Neolithic town at Çatalhöyük, occupied from the eighth to the sixth millennium BC. Painted images of hunters pursuing deer and other game adorned the walls of the mudbrick buildings. The decorative programme also included plastered bull skulls with their horns protruding. A celebrated figure of a mother goddess giving birth while seated on a throne made of lions was found at the site in a grain bin. The image of the female deity stationed upon or flanked by wild animals was never forgotten in the region.

Our story truly begins, however, in the Middle Bronze Age. At the start of the second millennium BC, the Old Assyrians established a number of trading colonies in Anatolia. The most notable of these *kārū* was the settlement of Kaneš, also known as Nesa (in the modern locale of Kültepe). The Assyrians offered tin (used in the production of bronze) and textiles. The gold and silver received from these transactions was sent back to their homeland. It was not only merchandise that the Assyrians brought to Anatolia but knowledge of writing. Thousands of letters found at the site document the communication between these remote merchants and their family members back in the Mesopotamian city-state of Assur. These tablets, although written in Old Assyrian, preserve the earliest traces of Hittite language in names and a handful of other words. The cuneiform script, in turn, came to be adopted by the peoples of Anatolia, allowing historical records to be produced in the region for the first time. Other than the clay tablets, the traders left few traces of their Assyrian heritage in Anatolia. The pottery and other elements of material culture at the site very much resemble that of the natives. After two hundred years of trading in the region, the Assyrians left in the mid-eighteenth century BC and seem to have taken their belongings with them.

Zoomorphic vessel from the period of the Assyrian trading colonies in Anatolia.

At the time of the Assyrian traders, the one major ethnic group in central Anatolia was the Hattians. They were organized as city-states. One of these small kingdoms was based at Hattus, which was to become the site of the future Hittite capital. In the eighteenth century BC a king named Pithana, of the city Kussara, conquered Kaneš and made it his capital. His son, Anitta, subsequently campaigned against and destroyed Hattus. Weeds were sown in its ruins and Anitta placed a curse on the site, such that it should remain uninhabited for all time. Anitta wrote this down in a record of his family's exploits, a document known as the Anitta Text. It is regarded as the oldest known text composed in the Hittite language, and its archaic syntax is preserved in copies made by later Hittite scribes. An additional inscription for this period was discovered on a spearhead at Kaneš, which identified the building from which it was excavated as 'the palace of Anitta the prince'.[1] Kaneš/Nesa became regarded by future generations of Hittites as their ancestral home, and they thus referred to their language as Nesite. It was once believed that the Hittites originated as a group of Indo-European speakers, who entered Anatolia and established supremacy over the Hattians. It seems more likely that native Hattians were gradually absorbed by the Hittites through their choice to adopt the Indo-European Nesite language. As a result, Hittite art, religion and culture contain many echoes of Hattian tradition. Hattic personal and place names also continued being used in the Hittite period. No documents composed in the Hattian language survive that were written by native speakers. It is in passages within Hittite text that excerpts of Hattic are preserved.

The Hittites were never a single-ethnicity identity, but rather a cultural conglomerate formed from an intermingling of peoples. In addition to the ruling dynasty who spoke the Hittite/Nesite language, Hatti was inhabited by other racial groups of Anatolian, Mesopotamian and Syrian origin. Hittitologist Trevor Bryce points out that

What gave them a recognizable common identity, in their own eyes and in the eyes of their neighbours, was not a common language, nor a common cultural or ethnic identity, but the fact that they lived within a clearly defined region which differentiated them from other subjects of the king who lived further afield in vassal states.[2]

Though a mixed population, they were all people of the land of Hatti.

## The first kings of the Hittites

Written tradition regarded Labarna (?–1650 BC) as the first king of the Hittites. Information about this early ruler is a little vague, but it appears that he initially ruled over one of the small kingdoms in north-central Anatolia, before subsequently conquering and absorbing several small states surrounding his own. 'On whatever campaign he went, he held the lands of the enemy in subjection by his might,' notes the later-composed Telipinu Proclamation.[3] It was Labarna who set the example of the warrior king for subsequent Hittite rulers. 'Labarna' became a title used by subsequent Hittite kings. His wife was the queen Tawananna, who, like her husband, lent her name as an honorific for future Hittite queens. The capital from which Labarna ruled was Kussar, the original base of Pithana. At present, its location has not been discovered.

Labarna's successor began his reign with the decision to move the capital to Hattusa, taking the throne name Hattusili to mark this significant event. From then on, he was the 'Man of Hattusa'. Some scholars have argued that Hattusili I (1650–1620 BC) was in fact Labarna, as the king referred to himself by this royal title prior to shifting the capital. Thus Anitta's curse ('May the Storm-god strike down anyone who becomes king after me and resettles Hattusa') upon the resettlement of the city was short-lived.[4] Refounding a city here – constructing a brand-new settlement, with all the facilities necessary to sustain and protect the people relocated to populate it – would have been a huge feat. So why did Hattusili instigate this move? Though exposed to severe environmental conditions, location on a large outcrop of rock provided excellent natural fortifications. Surrounding forest offered an abundance of timber, and Hattusa's seven springs assured a constant water supply. It was also an opportunity to forge a new identity, apparent in Hattusili's change of name alongside the refounding.

From his new capital, Hattusili I began conducting military campaigns against the kingdom of Yamhad in Syria. The important port city of Alalakh was sacked and destroyed. But further expedition was cut short by troubles back home. The territories of western Anatolia, known as the Arzawa Lands, commenced a series of raids on the Hittite border. Campaigns to quell problems in the west would become frequent ventures for the Hittites, even when part of this area was subject to vassalage. However, while Hattusili was dealing with the Arzawa Lands, the Hittite heartland was exposed to another force from the southeast: the Hurrians. A lack of manpower meant that this pattern, whereby the homeland was left exposed to invasion while military campaigns were being conducted, was all too frequent for the Hittites. Although Hattusili effectively drove out the invasion, the Hurrians would remain a military menace for much of Hittite history (as well as being highly influential on Hittite culture, as we will see). The most formidable of the Hurrian states was known as the Mittani. Hattusili's annals, which were originally inscribed on a gold statue of the king, describe all of his military domination over the aforementioned peoples. The document gives particular attention to the wagonloads of war booty that he brought home from campaigning – costly objects used to furnish his new capital. Hattusili even compares himself to Sargon the Great, the formidable Akkadian king who founded history's first empire after conquering the Sumerian city-states of Mesopotamia.

One issue remained for the Hittite monarch to resolve: choosing an appropriate heir and successor to the throne. A Hittite crown prince was known as a *Tuhkanti*. Hattusili's son Huzziya had been outposted as a regional governor and was likely first choice for the position. But his involvement in an uprising against the Hittite king saw him apprehended for treason. Hattusili's daughter (whose husband would qualify for the throne) was also banished for leading a revolt. He therefore decided to appoint his nephew as successor. The nephew likewise proved to be a poor choice for a *Tuhkanti*. He constantly ignored the king's instruction, preferring to heed bad advice from his mother, the king's sister. Hattusili described his sister as a wicked woman, calling her a 'serpent' who 'bellowed like an ox' on hearing that her son's succession appointment had been revoked.[5] Both sister and nephew were quickly banished.

Disheartened after being let down by his family, the king fell sick. A document known as the Testament of Hattusili describes his final appointment for the throne, made from his deathbed. Trevor Bryce notes the importance of this remarkable document, which 'is almost certainly a verbatim record of what the king actually said – not a later tidied-up and edited version of it, like most official documents of the kingdom . . . These are the very first preserved spoken words in an Indo-European language.'[6] Hattusili adopted his grandson, Mursili, and had him determined as successor. But Mursili was only a child, so as Hattusili lay dying, he advised him on behaviour appropriate for a monarch. Hattusili stipulated that these instructions were to be read out once per month to remind the boy king of his duties. His testament concluded with Hattusili expressing fear at his approaching death. Speaking to a woman named Hastayar (probably his wife or a concubine), he asked her to 'Wash me well, hold me to your breast, protect me from the earth.'[7] But even kings are not immune to the inevitable.

### From Mursili to Telipinu

Following Hattusili's death, kingship was bestowed upon the adopted grandson who ruled as Mursili I (1620–1590 BC). Mursili continued military campaigns against Hatti's neighbours. He achieved great feats, capturing and destroying both Aleppo and Babylon. This brought an end to the Babylonian dynasty founded almost three hundred years earlier by the famed law-giving king Hammurabi. The fall of the Old Babylonian Empire led to the establishment of the Kassites in Mesopotamia. Similarly, the Hittite's success in Syria led to the spread of the Hurrians, who filled the power vacuum. Following his return home from campaigning, Mursili was assassinated by his brother-in-law, Hantili, who then assumed the throne. Hantili I (1590–1560 BC) justified his act by claiming that Mursili's destruction of the great Near Eastern city of Babylon 'made the gods sick'.[8]

While warring with the Hurrians, Hantili's wife and children were captured and murdered by the enemy. Kingship then passed to Zidanta I, who dispatched any remaining heirs of Hantili at the time of the king's death. Zidanta ruled very briefly, before being assassinated by his own son Ammuna (1560–1525 BC). Although Ammuna himself died of natural causes, his sons were murdered by Huzziya I. It was in this turbulent environment that Telipinu (1525–1500 BC) became king of Hatti, seizing power from Huzziya in a bloodless coup. By now, struggles for the throne were a regular occurrence. The throne name Telipinu was unique among the Hittite kings and may have been deliberately chosen, as it was also the name of an agricultural deity who, in a myth, restored order to a world in chaos.

Concerned by the frequent conspiracies and bloodbaths that followed the death of early rulers, Telipinu established laws of succession for Hittite kings. The son of the king's first wife would assume the throne on that ruler's death. Should there be no son by the wife, then kingship should pass to the son of one of his concubines. If there was still no male heir, then a husband of one of his daughters could be adopted as his son. Telipinu was also the first king to begin to make use of diplomacy when dealing with international powers rather than pure military might. When negotiating with the Kizzuwatna, he opted for a treaty of alliance with its king, which allowed the state to retain independence. Kizzuwatna was in a key position, as a gateway between Hittite and Mittani territory. The Kizzuwatneans would use their strategic location to bargain with the two powers, switching allegiance between the opposing sides several times. Despite his efforts in establishing rules for succession, Telipinu left no heir at the time of his death: his only son had been murdered. A century of decline followed, marked by a series of ineffective rulers. The pattern of assassinations and usurpations continued.

## Allusions to the Hellenic Bronze Age: Ahhiyawa and Wilusa

The beginning of the Hittite New Kingdom is marked by the reign of Tudhaliya I/II, who became king circa 1400 BC. Tudhaliya's first military operations were directed towards the western kingdoms known as the Arzawa Lands. Included among them were the states of Hapalla, Wilusa, Mira and the Seha River Land. Of particular interest to scholars are the sparse and tantalizing references to Wilusa, most probably the Hittite name for Ilios, the legendary city of Troy. One such remark is preserved in a later document, called the Tawagalawa Letter, between an unnamed Hittite monarch and the king of another land called Ahhiyawa. The Ahhiyawans (a name linguistically similar to the Achaeans of Homer) have been identified by scholars as the Mycenaean Greeks. A statement in this letter suggests that the two kings had once fought over Wilusa until they reached an agreement. The archaeological layer of Troy VIIa, which is the most probable candidate for a Trojan War, existed contemporaneously to the Hittites. It was destroyed at the end of the thirteenth century, around the same time as the collapse of the empire and destruction of Hattusa. Whatever the case, the relationship between Bronze Age Wilusa and Homeric epic is far from clear. From at least the early thirteenth century, possibly earlier, Wilusa was nonetheless a Hittite subject state.

Arzawa had the potential to become a dangerous threat to the Hittites when they formed coalitions. One such confederacy of western states faced by Tudhaliya is referred to by modern scholars as the Assuwa league. Tudhaliya was victorious over this league of some 22 allied nations: the king boasted about bringing back and resettling 10,000 enemy infantry and six hundred of their chariotry, an act aimed at weakening the region. Though a rebellion was attempted by these deported troops, it was quickly put down and its instigator executed. A Mycenaean-style sword discovered near Hattusa in 1991 bears an inscription identifying it as an enemy weapon acquired as tribute from the Assuwa campaign. While Tudhaliya's military operations in the west were successful, they left the Hittite heartland yet again exposed to enemy forces. The Kaska (highland raiders from the north) invaded the kingdom.

Tudhaliya drove them out, only to face more trouble developing in the east. The troublesome Mittani had gained considerable influence over Syria. Tudhaliya's campaigns to deal with the threat proved profitable. Key Mittani strongholds were destroyed and the buffer state of Kizzuwatna was annexed, now falling under direct Hittite control.

Tudhaliya was succeeded by his son-in-law, Arnuwanda I. Connections with the west during this period are illuminated by a fascinating letter addressed from Arnuwanda to an individual named Madduwatta. The events documented in the *Indictment of Madduwatta* begin in the reign of Tudhaliya. Madduwatta, having fled from the court of an Ahhiyawan ruler named Attarsiya, sought protection in Hatti. As noted, the Ahhiyawans were likely the Mycenaeans of Bronze Age Greece, and some scholars have suggested the name Attarsiya was a Hittite rendering of the legendary king Atreus. Madduwatta had somehow made an enemy of Attarsiya and had been expelled. He must have been a person of some importance, for Tudhaliya had Madduwatta installed as a vassal ruler. He was given a mountainous region called Zippasla, which bordered the western lands of the Arzawa.

The ambitious Madduwatta began to extend the territory over which he held power, ignoring his obligations to the Hittite king. Forming his own small kingdom, he conquered much of western Anatolia and even invaded Alashiya (the Hittite name for Cyprus). He attempted to independently forge a diplomatic alliance, proposing a marriage between his daughter and the Arzawan king Kupanta-Kurunta. To the suspicious Hittite ruler, Madduwatta claimed this was simply an act that would allow the vassal to assassinate the king of Arzawa. On one occasion, Madduwatta's meddling in the region resulted in his own lands being invaded. Fleeing for his life, he required the Hittite king to come to the rescue. There was no retaliation from the Hittite monarch for Madduwatta's duplicitous behaviour, however, other than some strongly worded correspondence. This may seem surprising, but it reflects that, at this time, the Hittites were just not that interested in western expansion. Past campaigns in the west had exposed the Hittites' other borders to attack. In fact, the disobedient vassal may have been inadvertently acting in Hatti's interest simply by destabilizing the region. Though unruly, Madduwatta did not rise up against the Hittite state, so he was not a threat.

## An empire emerges from ashes

During Arnuwanda's reign the Kaska were once again causing havoc on Hatti's northern border. Particularly devastating was their sacking of many religious cities. In a prayer composed to the Hittite Sun-goddess, Arnuwanda laments: 'The Kaska-men destroyed your temples and smashed your images, O gods.'[9] Gold and silver offering vessels, as well as the garments worn by the gods, were plundered. The religious personnel were forced into the servitude of the Kaska. Hatti lacked the resources to respond effectively, and Arnuwanda's attempts to subdue the Kaska were of limited success, but during the reign of his son, King Tudhaliya III, it was not only the Kaska on the offensive. Hatti was at crisis point, overwhelmed by attacks on all borders in what has been called a 'concentric invasion'.[10] In correspondence between Egypt and the Arzawan king, Pharaoh Amenhotep III wrote: 'I have heard that everything is finished, and that the country Hattusa is paralyzed.'[11] The Hittite capital was abandoned and Tudhaliya III temporarily moved the remnants of the state to a settlement called Samuha. Recent archaeological evidence has identified Samuha as probably being modern Kayalıpınar, located in the Sivas province of eastern Turkey. A notable discovery from this site was made in 2005 of a relief depicting a seated goddess holding a drinking cup in one hand and a bird in the other; she is sat upon a throne with legs that terminate in lion's paws. The Hittite's vision of civilization was unwilling to die just yet. From this place of refuge at Samuha, the king began working to re-establish dominion over Anatolia.

It was an effort that took some twenty years. Military campaigns were conducted against both the Kaska in the north and the Arzawa in the west. The reconquered Hittite cities, which had been ravaged by these enemy forces, were refortified and repopulated. Much of the military action was managed by Tudhaliya's son and closest adviser, Suppiluliuma. And yet, when the now-sickly king died in Samuha, it was not Suppiluliuma who was appointed to succeed him. Tudhaliya III's older son, known as Tudhaliya the Younger, had been designated as heir. The ambitious Suppiluliuma was discontented by the position being handed to his older brother, and so were a number of people in the court. Suppiluliuma had already proved himself on the battlefield. It was this type of personality that the nation needed to restore Hittite control in Anatolia and expand its borders. With the support of the army, the heir was assassinated, and Suppiluliuma I (1350–1322 BC) became the new Hittite monarch. He would rise to become the Hittites' greatest military leader.

Suppiluliuma's campaigns focused on expanding southeast into Syria. His main opponent civilization was the Mittani. Though Suppiluliuma sacked the capital city, Washukanni, the Mittani king, Tushratta, fled and was to prove an elusive problem for the Hittites. This king was quite a character. In a series of letters written by Tushratta he complains he has been sent a gift from Egypt of two gold-plated wooden statues, rather than solid gold ones. He requests that next time the pharaoh should send him 'much gold', for in Egypt 'gold is as plentiful as dirt'.[12] In order to undermine Tushratta, Suppiluliuma allied himself with a rival claimant to the Mittanian throne. An alliance was also formed with the Syrian kingdom of Ugarit. It was a coveted land, rich in agricultural production and timber, and eventually became a prized Hittite vassal state. As Suppiluliuma progressed on his expeditions, the kings (and their families) of the conquered states and cities were deported to the Hittite capital. Victory over two key Syrian cities saw them placed under direct Hittite rule. One of Suppiluliuma's sons, Telipinu, was made viceroy of Aleppo. Following the conquest of Carchemish, another son named Piyassili was installed as its viceroy. The brothers' administration in the region allowed Suppiluliuma to return home and deal with the Kaska, who were once again raiding Hatti from the north. The fall of Carchemish to the Hittites essentially marked the end for the Mittani. Soon after, the ever-fleeing Tushratta was assassinated by his own people. The remains of the weakened Mittani state were quickly dominated by a new power on the international stage: the Middle Assyrian Empire.

A third son of Suppiluliuma, Zannanza, was sent to Egypt. He had been requested as a husband by a distressed Egyptian queen, who felt vulnerable on becoming suddenly widowed. Zannanza was assassinated while on his way to forge this diplomatic alliance, which would have seen the Hittite prince become pharaoh. We will examine this episode more closely in our discussion of international relations in the next chapter. The incident led to retaliatory invasion by Suppiluliuma into Egyptian-occupied territories. The prisoners of war brought back from these campaigns to Hatti carried plague with them. The epidemic was to devastate the Hittite homeland for the next two decades and included Suppiluliuma among its victims. His son Arnuwanda II, who succeeded him, also contracted the plague and died after a short reign. Suppiluliuma's youngest son, Mursili II (1321–1295 BC), then became king.

## The successes and suffering of Mursili II

Mursili's military ventures focused largely on the conquest of the Arzawan states in the west. Assisted by his brother Piyassili, the viceroy of Carchemish, these lands were finally brought under Hittite control. A population of some 65,000 people were supposedly deported and resettled in Hatti. This effective technique, which was used by Hittite kings on multiple occasions to deal with subject territories, served two functions: it weakened the resources of a newly conquered region, to reduce the probability of future uprisings, and provided a much-needed population boost in the Hittite heartland. As a result, the homeland became a cultural conglomerate of peoples. Vassal rulers were installed to govern the regions of Hapalla, Mira and the Seha River Land in western Anatolia.

The imperial ambitions of Egypt and Assyria were kept in check by the two viceregal seats in the region, being effectively managed by Mursili's older brothers. When both Telipinu and Piyassili died in the same year, however, Hittite control in Syria was destabilized. The Assyrians quickly invaded and took Carchemish. Mursili drove them out, restoring Hittite authority in the region, with the placement of Piyassili's son as viceroy of Carchemish and Telipinu's son as viceroy of Aleppo. Mursili made little more progress than his predecessors in subduing the pesky Kaska in the north. A small victory was the temporary recapture of the sacred city of Nerik back from the Kaska. Mursili was the first Hittite monarch to worship at its temples in two hundred years.

Despite these successes, the empire that Mursili had inherited from Suppiluliuma came with some serious problems that quite literally plagued his reign. The disease brought to Hatti during Suppiluliuma's rule continued to infect the homeland and reduce the population. Mursili consulted the gods via oracles to find out what had caused the plague that was ravaging his country. Through his enquiries the king discovered that the disease was a divine punishment afflicted on Hatti for the crimes of his father. The pestilence was believed to be a lingering pollution originating from Suppiluliuma's murder of the legitimate heir to the Hittite throne, Tudhaliya the Younger. Suppiluliuma's failure to give offerings to the Mala (Euphrates) River, as well as the violation of a treaty, were also cited as reasons for the spread of the disease.

Responding to the desperate situation, Mursili enacted rituals and begged the gods for forgiveness in a series of so-called 'plague prayers'. These compositions are regarded as some of the most emotive in the corpus of Hittite literature. Mursili's prayers feel very human as he pleads with and attempts to placate an uncontrollable force.

> May the gods, my lords, again be well disposed towards me, and let me elicit your pity. May you listen to me, to what I plead before you. I have not done any evil. Of those who sinned and did the evil, no one of that day is still here. They have already died off. But because the affair of my father has come upon me, I am giving you, O gods, my lords, a propitiatory gift on account of the plague of the land, and I am making restitution ... Send away the worry from my heart, take away the anguish from my soul.[13]

He compares himself to a bird that seeks refuge in a cage, an analogy for protection sought from the gods. The king even offered bribes in the form of the restoration of religious sanctuaries and the gods' images: 'For whatever god there is no temple, I will build a temple for him. And whichever gods have been destroyed, I restore for them a statue.'[14] Mursili requested that if any further compensation was required of him, the gods should reveal it in his dreams.

In the prayers, the king complained that the plague had left his land vulnerable to the hostility of enemies – the Mittani, Kaska and Arzawans – who did not worship Hittite gods and wished to despoil their temples. Mursili suggested the gods should actually redirect the plague upon these nations instead. The king reasoned with the gods that the situation would also have repercussions in the divine sphere: 'If the gods, my lords, do not remove the plague from Hatti, the makers of offering bread and libation pourers will keep on dying. And if they too die, the offering bread and libations will be cut off from the gods.'[15] The cuneiform tablet on which one of the prayers is written bears the instruction that it was to be read aloud to the gods on a daily basis. The texts do not describe any of the disease's symptoms. While Mursili did not contract the plague, he was struck down with another ailment: during his reign the king was afflicted with speech paralysis, possibly resulting from a stroke. A substitution ritual was performed in an attempt to transfer the affliction from the king.

Another problem introduced by Suppiluliuma was also having reverberations during Mursili's reign. For an unknown reason, Suppiluliuma dismissed his wife, Henti. Mursili's mother was banished and replaced by a new wife from Babylon. The Babylonian Tawananna outlived her husband Suppiluliuma, and proved to be a domineering force during the reign of her stepson. She retained power at the Hittite court, introducing unwelcome foreign customs from Babylon and lavishing riches from the palace upon her favourites. Mursili begrudgingly put up with her extravagance, but the final affront occurred when the Babylonian Tawananna targeted Mursili's own wife, Gassulawiya: 'She stands day and night before the gods and curses my wife before the gods . . . she wishes for her death saying: "Let her die".'[16] It was then that Gassulawiya suddenly fell ill with a mysterious illness.

In prayer, Mursili pleaded with the gods to save his beloved wife: 'Accept, O god, this offering in good spirit and turn again in favour to Gassulawiya. Save her from this sickness! Take it away from her and let her recover! Then it will come to pass that in the future Gassulawiya will constantly praise you.'[17] But his efforts proved futile, and, soon after, Gassulawiya died. The 'evil step-mother' was accused of witchcraft. She was placed on trial, found guilty and banished from the capital. The heartbroken Mursili II evidently missed Gassulawiya and lamented that, 'throughout the days of life my soul goes down to the dark Netherworld on her account.'[18] He may have remarried a woman named Danuhepa, but it seems more likely that this individual was a wife of Mursili's son and successor, Muwatalli II. Much like the Babylonian Tawananna, Danuhepa's influence in the capital proved undesirable. For reasons that are unclear, she fell out of favour, was placed on trial and was subsequently banished by Muwatalli II.

### War and peace with Egypt: Muwatalli II and Hattusili III

Muwatalli II (1295–1272 BC) began his reign by moving the Hittite capital from Hattusa to a new settlement named Tarhuntassa, located somewhere in southern Anatolia. Hittite sources claim this was on instruction of the Storm-god, but still the decision to move the seat of kingship is a surprising one. For 350 years Hattusa had been at the heart of the Hittites. When the city had previously been captured, it had been imperative to get it back. Perhaps the move to Tarhuntassa was to distance the administrative centre of the empire from the Kaska raiders in the north. Or maybe it was to prepare for the upcoming battles in Syria with Egypt. It could be that Muwatalli had designs to give more attention to the temples of the south, which had often been neglected in favour of the northern religious institutions. Hattusa was not completely abandoned and continued functioning as a regional centre for northern Anatolia. The north was administered by Muwatalli's brother, who would later become King Hattusili III. Although the ancestral spirits and gods were transferred to Tarhuntassa (signifying this was intended as a permanent relocation), they were restored to Hattusa following Muwatalli's death. This, however, was not to be the end of Tarhuntassa. It remained an important city which would later become a rebel base for resistance against kingship in Hattusa.

During this period, tension between Egypt and the Hittites over contested territory in Syria had reached breaking point. Amurru and Qadesh were formerly under Egyptian control but had now been annexed by the Hittites. Clashes between the two powers culminated in a showdown that has come to define Muwatalli's reign: the Battle of Qadesh. The year was 1274 BC. On one side of this war was Muwatalli and the mighty Hittite troops; on the other was the huge Egyptian army, led by the great warrior pharaoh Ramesses II. A detailed account of the battle survives via Egyptian sources, monumentally recorded by Ramesses on the walls of five different Egyptian temples. The Hittite army was reported to be composed of some 47,500 troops recruited from across the empire, including 3,500 chariotry. Both Mutawalli and his brother Hattusili III were among the commanders on the Hittite side at the battle. Ramesses' troops were divided into four main units, each named after an Egyptian god: Amun, Ra, Ptah and Seth. The Amun division was at the head of the advance from Egypt into Syria, led by the pharaoh himself. As they progressed, these Egyptian troops were approached by two men claiming to be defectors of the Hittite army. They reported that the Hittites were still far away, in the north at Aleppo. Ramesses did not verify the story and the Amun division began to set up camp near the city of Qadesh, on the western side of the Orontes River. He would soon learn, however, that the two men were spies sent by Muwatalli to mislead the Egyptians, when two actual Hittite units, sent to do a reconnaissance of the Egyptian position, were captured. Under torture they divulged that the Hittite army was in fact nearby, concealed on the other side of the Orontes River.

The Hittite army attacked and scattered the troops of Amun as the Egyptians were still setting up camp. En route they also attacked the second division of Ra, who were approaching from the south. Ramesses dispatched messengers to hurry the other divisions, the Ptah and Seth troops being still too far away to assist the Egyptian effort. At this point the Hittite troops, believing their victory was imminent, abandoned discipline. They began to plunder the Egyptian camp, their chariots weighed down with booty. This gave the Egyptians the opportunity to regroup, and when reinforcements arrived, the pharaoh's army was able to push back the Hittites. The Egyptian temple walls list the names of the Hittite commanders slaughtered in the conflict. The pharaoh retreated southwards, with the Hittites pursuing the Egyptian army as far as Damascus. While the Egyptians claimed victory, the battle ultimately resulted in a draw. The outcomes certainly favoured the Hittites: the coveted states of Qadesh and Amurru remained under Hittite control. They also now occupied Damascus, although this territory was later given back to the Egyptians.

A treaty was drawn up some fifteen years following the Battle of Qadesh (during Hattusili III's reign), declaring an 'eternal' peace between the two powers. In it, the Hittites and Egyptians agreed not to invade each other. Boundaries were drawn for maintaining harmony in the contested area of Syria, and a clause of the treaty required both parties to support each other against attack from a third party or internal rebellion. It also included a stipulation commonly found in treaties that obligated the signatories to return fugitives who fled into their territory. The Hittite version of the document curiously contained a clause absent from the Egyptian version. It stipulated that the pharaoh would acknowledge Hattusili's descendants as kings of Hatti. This was a reflection of Hattusili's desire to secure succession for his heirs, following his ascent to kingship via usurpation (as will be explained shortly). Both the Hittite version and the Egyptian version survive antiquity. The version composed in the Hittite court was sent to Ramesses and then translated into Egyptian. He had it engraved in hieroglyphs on the walls of two temples in Thebes.[19] The Egyptian version, which was delivered to the Hittite capital, was written in Akkadian. The original document was engraved on a silver tablet, a clay copy of which has been discovered at Hattusa. Today, a replica of this cuneiform version of the treaty hangs prominently on a wall of the United Nations Headquarters in New York – an attempt to remind world leaders of the possibility of peace between vying international powers.

Akkadian cuneiform version of the Egyptian–Hittite peace treaty found at Hattusa.

Egyptian–Hittite peace treaty engraved in hieroglyphs on the temple walls at Karnak.

At the end of Muwatalli II's reign, his son Urhi-Teshub (1272–1267 BC) became king. With the restoration of Hattusa as the Hittite capital, Hattusili III (who had been governing the northern regions for his brother Muwatalli) was stripped of his powers. Conflict soon erupted between uncle and nephew, with Hattusili III (1267–1237 BC) ultimately attaining kingship of Hatti. Urhi-Teshub was exiled. Sickly as a child, Hattusili had not been expected to reach adulthood. He was placed in a temple as a servant of the goddess Ishtar (also known by the Hurrio-Hittite name Šauška), who was credited with saving him. She remained Hattusili's patron throughout his life and was reported to have overseen his successes and legitimized his decisions. During the power struggle for kingship, Ishtar had apparently acknowledged him as the rightful monarch, appearing before Urhi-Teshub's generals in dreams and converting them to Hattusili's side. Prior to becoming king, Hattusili had married the daughter of a priest of Ishtar from the city of Lawazantiya, an important cult centre of the goddess. 'The goddess gave us the love of husband and wife,' writes Hattusili. 'In the house which we made ourselves, the goddess was there with us and our house thrives.'[20] Her name was Puduhepa.

Puduhepa became the most notable of the Hittite queens. Much more than simply a consort, she wielded considerable power. The queen co-signed treaties with her husband, including the famed peace treaty with Egypt that resulted from the Battle of Qadesh. Puduhepa assisted with reorganizing the ever-increasing Hittite pantheon, which acquired new gods whenever territory was added to the empire. This saw some amalgamation of deities, whom she recognized to be multiple versions of the same god: 'Sun-goddess of Arinna, you are Queen of all countries! In the land of Hatti you bear the name of the Sun-goddess of Arinna; but in the land which you made the cedar land you bear the name Hebat.'[21] Diplomatic relations were a key feature of Hattusili's reign, to which the queen made valuable contributions. Puduhepa organized marriage alliances with foreign powers, exemplified in direct correspondence exchanged between herself and Ramesses II. The pharaoh complained to her of delays in receiving his Hittite princess. Puduhepa responded by reproaching the Egyptian king for only being interested in the gifts that would accompany the marriage.

An impression of Puduhepa's seal, found at Hattusa, attests to her role in economic activities. Her involvement in the exchange of goods is exhibited in a legal case against an official named Ura-Tarhunta.[22] He had been tasked with overseeing a delivery of goods owned and sealed by Puduhepa. The queen accused him of embezzlement of these resources when several items disappeared en route to Babylonia. Among the offences he admitted to was exchanging several of Puduhepa's mules, which she had lent out to him at a profit, with his own mules (which were likely much inferior to those owned by the queen). Ura-Tarhunta had also purloined for himself a male and a female slave from a group of captives owned by Puduhepa. As a result of the trial, the queen announced a concession that any old items no longer required by the crown could freely be claimed by her officials. These included textiles and chariots. Access to these goods provided an incentive for officials to act loyally in their ventures undertaken on behalf of the queen. Objects made of precious metals were excluded, as they could be recast and retained a continuing value.

Hattusili and Puduhepa's marriage proved a highly successful one, a partnership both loving and politically well-functioning. The king depended on her in frequent periods of sickness throughout his reign. During such times, she composed heartfelt pleas to the gods on his behalf. A depiction of both Puduhepa and Hattusili III survives in the Fıraktın relief, carved upon the rockface of a steep valley near the modern city of Kayseri. It is divided into two sections. On the left, a male scene portrays the king making an offering to the Storm-god. Hattusili is dressed in the likeness of this god, pouring a libation before an altar between them. On the right, in the female scene, Queen Puduhepa directs her libation towards the seated Sun-goddess. The solar deity holds up a cup in her hand. Names are identified above in Luwian hieroglyphs. The Fıraktın relief depicts the ideology of the Hittite king and queen as earthly representatives for the king and queen of the Hittite pantheon. In the parallel scenes Puduhepa and Hattusili are illustrated performing their roles equally and independently.

The Fıraktın relief.

Puduhepa continued to play a prominent role at court after the death of her much older husband.

### Towards decline

Puduhepa and Hattusili's son Tudhaliya IV (1237–1209 BC) was the next Hittite monarch. It is Tudhaliya who is represented among the gods at the famed rock-cut sanctuary at Yazılıkaya. The shrine began receiving embellishment as part of Tudhaliya's religious policy that saw the restoration of festivals and images of the gods that had fallen into neglect. The need for divine favour was especially high in his reign, which was beset with challenges. Several military campaigns were required to suppress unrest in the west of the empire, stirred up by the Ahhiyawans.

Tudhaliya's most powerful adversary, however, was to be the Assyrians. When a new Assyrian king, Tukulti-ninurta I, ascended the throne, both powers seemed initially intent on improving uneasy relations with each other. Tukulti-ninurta and Tudhaliya expressed friendship in the letters exchanged between them. The chance of peace between the powers immediately soured, however, when the Assyrians invaded Hurrian territories, which were now under Hittite control. The strained relations saw Tudhaliya implement the world's first trade embargo, which forbade trade between the ships of the Ahhiyawans and the Assyrians at the port of Amurru. Tensions culminated in a battle between the Assyrians and Hittites at Nihriya. The result was a humiliating defeat for Tudhaliya, whose allies deserted him when he needed them most. The Hittite king reprimanded one of these spineless vassals: 'As the situation turned difficult for me, you kept yourself somewhere away from me. Beside me you were not.'[23] Meanwhile, Tukulti-ninurta wrote boastfully of his victory in a letter to the king of Ugarit, likely in an attempt to drive a wedge in the allegiance between the Syrian vassal state and the Hittites. After the defeat at Nihriya, Ugarit certainly acted with more audacity towards Hatti.

The campaigns of Tudhaliya IV saw the successful invasion of Cyprus ('Alashiya') and the island becoming a Hittite tributary. Tudhaliya reported that the Cypriot king and his family were imprisoned and deported to the Hittite homeland. It is rather remarkable they even made the attempt, given that the Hittites were not seafaring people. Such a venture relied on the naval fleets of tributary and allied states. It is most likely that Amurru and Ugarit were called upon to ferry Hittite ambitions across the Mediterranean. It is unclear what prompted the Hittites to make the attack. Was it retaliatory? Or was it, perhaps, aimed at securing access to Cyprus's famed copper supplies? Hatti was becoming increasingly dependent on reliable trade routes, since resources were starting to deplete at home. Whatever the case, this alleged control over Cyprus was short-lived. In the reign of Tudhaliya IV's son Suppiluliuma II, the Hittites once again staged an invasion of the island that reportedly reduced it to the status of subject territory. Suppiluliuma's account of the naval battles off the coast of Cyprus are the first records in history of combat at sea. Despite such records, the Hittites left little archaeological evidence of their presence on Cyprus.

Tudhaliya's claim to the throne was not completely secure and faced some opposition, given his father had acquired kingship by unorthodox means. There was even a failed assassination attempt on Tudhaliya's life by an individual named Hesni. But it is another emerging figure that most intrigues scholars, one who appears to have developed ambitions for Hatti's throne. This supposed rival claimant was a man named Kurunta (also referred to as Kuruntiya). He was the son of Muwatalli II and brother of the usurped king Urhi-Teshub. Kurunta had been placed under the care of Hattusili III (during the period prior to kingship while he was managing the northern half of the empire). Tudhaliya and Kurunta had thus grown up together; they bore respect and affection for each other. During the power struggle, Kurunta had sided with his uncle, Hattusili III, rather than his brother. He was rewarded by being installed as the vassal ruler of Tarhuntassa. Amity continued during the reign of Tudhaliya, who drew up a new treaty with Kurunta. The document was inscribed on a bronze tablet and reaffirmed Kurunta's power over Tarhuntassa, stating that he could choose his own successor. It also noted a reduction in taxes he was required to pay to the capital.

Other evidence, however, may indicate that Kurunta was not content to have authority over just Tarhuntassa. Several seal impressions bearing his name, found at Hattusa, suggest he may have had other aspirations, for he began using the title 'Great King', a label reserved for the supreme Hittite monarch. At Hatip, a rock relief of a warrior god armed with a bow, spear and short sword also has the accompanying inscription: 'Kurunta, Great King, son of Muwatalli, Great King, Hero'.[24] This suggests that by assuming the title, Kurunta was attempting to make claim for the kingship of Hatti. It has been theorized that he might have been using Tarhuntassa as a base for building resistance against sovereignty in Hattusa.[25] By independently declaring Tarhuntassa to once again be the seat of the Hittite throne, he may have sought to install himself as its legitimate heir. His brother, after all, was the deposed king Urhi-Teshub. Another possibility is that rule over the empire was willingly divided between cousins Tudhaliya IV and Kurunta. On one occasion, Tudhaliya sent a distressed letter to Ramesses II requesting that he dispatch Egyptian physicians to assist an unwell Kurunta. Whether this was before or after the latter began using the honorific of 'Great King' is unknown. Tarhuntassa, the seat of this rival branch of the royal family, remains undiscovered. Perhaps one day its excavation will shed more light on this intriguing plot that seems to have destabilized Hatti as the divided state advanced towards its final days.

## The last king of the Hittites and the Bronze Age collapse

The last king of the Hittites was Suppiluliuma II (1207–1178 BC), who assumed the throne after the short reign of his brother, Arnuwanda III. It was Suppiluliuma II that abandoned Hattusa early in the twelfth century BC. Hatti's final days were marked with invasions, famine and unrest. The Egyptian pharaoh Merneptah reported that, following requests from the Hittites, grain was sent to Anatolia 'to keep alive the land of Hatti'.[26] A letter expressing urgent distress ('It is a matter of life or death') was likewise dispatched to Ugarit demanding a ship for the transportation of grain. The widespread famine saw Hatti demanding increased tribute from its vassals. To meet such demands, people in the Syrian city of Emar were driven to sell their children. Unable to fulfil the orders of their overlords, the vassal system began to break down. Climate change forced many of these populations to relocate in order to survive drought-induced food shortages.

In this growing atmosphere of desperation, Suppiluliuma committed to the construction of several religious monuments around Hattusa – a petition to the gods and his ancestors. Luwian hieroglyphic inscriptions upon them boast of his apparent achievements. In addition to the aforementioned naval attack on Cyprus, they recount that Suppiluliuma campaigned against Tarhuntassa. This conquest was likely aimed at reasserting authority and overthrowing the regime of the rival kingdom, which may have been becoming increasingly intent on the invasion of Hattusa itself. Any attempts to restore Hatti to its former glory, however, proved futile. Hattusa was soon evacuated by the Hittites. Packing up their belongings, Suppiluliuma II and his court fled. The site had already long been deserted by the time it was set aflame. To where the Hittites journeyed (and whether they actually arrived) is unknown. Their documentation simply ends.

The Hittite Empire was not alone in its disintegration. Many contemporary civilizations in the Near East and around the

The last king of the Hittite Empire, Suppiluliuma II, depicted on the walls of the Südburg structure at Hattusa.

Mediterranean toppled in the early twelfth century BC, a period that has become known as the Bronze Age collapse. The Mycenaean kingdoms of Greece, the Kassites of Babylonia and notable Syrian states like Ugarit were among the victims. While Egypt ultimately survived, the end of the New Kingdom saw rule in the Nile Valley fall into a period of decline. The cause of the destruction has often been attributed to the rampage of a mysterious group of invaders, referred to in Egyptian sources, that have become known as the Sea Peoples. There are many (inconclusive) theories as to their identity, from the Mycenaeans to the Philistines. It is likely that they were a collection of various refugee peoples who were forced to migrate in the increasingly turbulent environment that developed at the end of the Bronze Age.

Whether the Sea Peoples were responsible for the destruction layers found at many of the major Bronze Age palatial centres remains hotly debated. For Hattusa, it was more likely the Kaska, who eventually torched the city, and even this was after the site had already been abandoned. The Bronze Age 'collapse' should be viewed as gradual, rather than a sudden cataclysmic event. What seems most likely is that the downfall of these civilizations was the result of a variety of factors: the cumulative effect of changes in climate (resulting in famine), internal rebellion and invasions. Eric H. Cline tackles the Bronze Age collapse in the highly recommended book *1177 BC: The Year Civilization Collapsed*. One possible explanation he gives is the idea of a systems collapse:

> Perhaps the inhabitants could have survived one disaster, such as an earthquake or a drought, but they could not survive the combined effects of earthquake, drought, and invaders in rapid succession. A 'domino effect' then ensued, in which the disintegration of one civilization led to the fall of the others.[27]

Given the interconnectedness of civilizations at the end of the Bronze Age, the demise of one society had economic ramifications on all others as trading networks between them became disrupted.

The empire may have crumbled, but some Hittite traditions continued for another five hundred years. The advent of the Iron Age saw the emergence of states in northern Syria and southern Anatolia that retained aspects of Hittite culture. We will return to these so-called Neo-Hittites in Chapter Eight. Now that we have met the Hittite kings, we will flesh out the world in which they lived. The next few sections of this book will thematically explore the various customs and characteristics that made up Hittite society: their art, their religion, their settlements, how they organized themselves as a civilization and how they responded during encounters with other nations.

# THREE

# VIA DIPLOMACY OR WAR: HITTITE INTERNATIONAL RELATIONS

I n this chapter we will thematically examine common trends
in the way the Hittites dealt with other civilizations. In their
Anatolian heartland, the kings of Hatti were encircled by other
powers. To the north were the Kaska raiders. To the southeast
was Kizzuwatna. This was the access point to Syria, domain of
the Hurrian kingdom of Mittani. The Arzawa Lands lay to the
southwest, and included such allied kingdoms as the Seha River
Land, Mira and Wilusa (Troy). Further west were the lands of
the Ahhiyawans (Mycenaean Greeks) and Alashiya (Cyprus).
And then there was Egypt. The Egyptians initially fought with
the Mittani over territory in the Levant, but in time they united
against the Hittites. Through a combination of battles, marriage
alliances and treaties the Hittites balanced their position in this
world. Negotiation and subjugation kept foreign powers in check
and allowed for the expansion of Hittite-controlled territory.
Success in both diplomacy and warfare was indeed profitable for
the state, supporting a steady flow of commodities in the form of
gifts, tribute and booty.

## Diplomacy

A wealth of information is available on Hittite interactions
with neighbouring powers during the fourteenth century BC.

Cuneiform documents from this period, particularly those found at Akhenaten's capital of Amarna in Egypt, provide a record for this era of international diplomacy. The rulers of the great Near Eastern powers, including the Babylonians, Assyrians, Mittani and Egyptians, as well as the Hittites, wrote letters to one another. One of these texts intriguingly included the ruler of the Ahhiyawa among these 'Great Kings'. The letters were written in Akkadian, the international language of the time. In their correspondence, rulers referred to each other as 'brother' or, more occasionally, adopted a father–son relationship. One Hittite king bluntly rejected such formalities in a curt reply to a letter from the ruler of Assyria: 'On what account should I write to you about brotherhood? Were you and I born from one mother?'[1]

The Amarna Letters record the exchange of gifts, diplomatic marriages, news of current events and quarrels among these competing civilizations. They include letters that refer to the Hittites or were written directly by the Hittite king. One letter recounts that a Hittite prince named Zita had sent sixteen men as a greeting gift to an Egyptian king. Zita requested reciprocation, not-so-subtly declaring he was 'desirous of gold'.[2] In another, the Egyptian pharaoh complained that the Canaanite ruler Aziru had provided for the messenger of the Hittite king, while ignoring his own Egyptian messenger.[3] Particularly prevalent are letters from rulers of cities and small kingdoms of the Levant, vassals of Egypt, expressing concern to the pharaoh about the military power of the Hittites. They plea for troops as the approaching Hittites set cities aflame. A document from Amarna reports that the small state of Nuhašše rejected an alliance with the Hittites in favour of staying loyal to Egypt.[4] A later text notes the outcome: the Hittite king seized and took up residence in Nuhašše, much to the fear of neighbouring regions.[5]

One of the most interesting examples of correspondence from this age of diplomacy comes from outside the Amarna archive. It was found at the Hittite capital of Hattusa. Suppiluliuma I received an unexpected letter from the Egyptian queen Ankhesenamun. The distressed queen chose to send a letter to Hatti when she found herself in a vulnerable position after the sudden death of

One of the Amarna Letters. This particular tablet (EA 23) is addressed from King Tushratta of the Mittani to the pharaoh. It reports that the cult statue of the goddess Šauška/Ishtar is being sent to the Nile Valley to aid the health of the Egyptian king. In the document, the Hurrio-Hittite goddess says, 'I wish to go to Egypt, a country that I love, and then return.'

her husband, the famous pharaoh Tutankhamun. Her letter to the Hittite king reads: 'My husband has died, and I have no son. They say you have many sons. If you will give me one of your sons, he will become my husband. I do not wish to choose a subject of mine and make him my husband. I am afraid.'[6] Suppiluliuma cautiously investigated the situation, as it was unprecedented for Egypt to willingly place a foreigner on the throne. The Egyptians held a long-standing belief that the Hittites and other non-Egyptian peoples were inferior to themselves. Documents from the Amarna archive illustrate that while royal women from the great Near Eastern empires were sent to Egypt to forge diplomatic alliances through marriages, Egyptian pharaohs consistently avoided recip-rocation and declined sending their own daughters abroad. To Suppiluliuma, Ankhesenamun's suggestion must have looked like an incredible opportunity to add the valuable land of Egypt to the Hittite dominion. The amazed Hittite king was recorded to have exclaimed, 'Nothing like this has ever happened to me in my whole life.'[7] But it was too good to be true. While negotiations resulted in the Hittite prince Zannanza being sent to Egypt, this son of Suppiluliuma was murdered when he reached the Nile Valley. Ankhesenamun (possibly pressured into doing so) was then married to Tutankhamun's successor, Ay. The new pharaoh, responding to angry letters from Suppiluliuma, denied that the prince had been assassinated. The incident resulted in raids by the Hittites on Egyptian settlements in Canaan and northern Syria. Disease that spread during these campaigns resulted in the death of Suppiluliuma himself, who became infected with plague.

Among the flurry of letters exchanged between the ancient monarchs, gifts were expected from fellow 'brother' kings when a new ruler ascended the throne. Therefore, Hattusili III complained to the king of Assyria, that 'When I assumed kingship, you did not send a messenger to me. It is the custom that when kings assume kingship, the kings, his equal in rank, send him appropriate gifts of greeting, clothing befitting kingship, and fine oil for his anointing. But you did not do this today.'[8] The exchange of gifts allowed kings to access many prestigious goods unavailable locally. Royal gift exchange was part of a much broader system of trade interactions in the ancient Near East. Hittite queens evidently also corresponded and shared presents with their foreign counterparts. The Egyptian queen Nefertari referred to Puduhepa as her 'sister' in a letter accompanying gifts of an elaborate twelve-band necklace of pure gold and garments of linen.

A repeated demand by Hittite monarchs in foreign correspondence was that his daughters used in marriage alliances be made chief wife of a recipient king. Thus, Puduhepa wrote brazenly to Ramesses II: 'Regarding the daughter that I will give to my brother . . . I want to make her superior to all the other daughters of Great Kings; no one should be able to find (another) beside her!'[9] A chief wife was responsible for producing the heir to the throne. The union of such a marriage could therefore result in a half-Hittite becoming pharaoh of Egypt. Ramesses did in fact fulfil the wishes of Puduhepa and Hattusili. Initially at least. Great honour was conferred upon the Hittite princess, who was given the Egyptian name Maat-Hor-Neferure ('One who sees Horus, the Visible Splendour of Re'). This wife, however, failed to produce a child. A frustrated Hattusili blamed Ramesses' virility in a letter to the pharaoh. The childless Hittite princess, having fallen from favour, then disappears from the historic record.

## The Hittite war machine

When diplomacy was not possible, there was always the formidable Hittite army. Hittite society valued military prowess and revolved around regular campaigning outside of the winter months. Trevor Bryce succinctly asserts, 'Fighting one's enemies was as regular and natural an activity among the Hittites as cultivating the soil and worshipping the gods . . . War, not peace, was the normal state of affairs. There was no ideology of peace.'[10] The gods oversaw the outcome of warfare and were said to accompany the king on the battlefield. For some kings this was quite literal rather than symbolic, and they reported instances of divine intervention in their accounts of battles. While Hittite kings were clearly proud of their military achievements, they did not exhibit the brutality towards their defeated enemies characteristic of the Assyrians.

The king was commander-in-chief and regularly accompanied his army on campaigns. Other members of the royal family sometimes attended military operations in his place, especially when campaigns were happening simultaneously in several different regions. Hittite princes were frequently installed in the prominent military appointment of the *gal geštin*, a title meaning 'chief of the wine'. The title probably had its origin as the position of trusted cupbearer, responsible for guarding the life of the king. By the period of the empire, these duties were remodelled into safeguarding the Hittite army. The *gal geštin* was often required to campaign independently on behalf of the king. Hatti's security was monitored via a series of garrisons positioned atop high ridges, capable of providing advanced warning of approaching enemy attack. Managing these fortresses was among the responsibilities of district governors across the empire known as *Bel Madgalti* ('Lord of the Watch Tower'). Silos were also set up at regular intervals across the empire to restock food rations that travelled with the ever-hungry army.

Two main types of troops made up the Hittite army: infantry (an estimated 90 per cent) and chariotry (approximately 10 per cent). The Hittites were particularly renowned for their elite circle of charioteers. The oldest equestrian training manual, written by an individual named Kikkuli, was found at Hattusa. It documents the diet, exercise regime and culling process that ensured chariot horses had optimum speed, strength and stamina for the battlefield. The rigorous 214-day programme even included a series of night-time drills to prepare horses for being alert and responsive in the event of nocturnal military operations. The carriages these animals pulled were made of a wooden frame stretched with animal hides. Hittite chariots modified the standard position of the wheel axle typical of other Near Eastern civilizations, moving it from the rear to the centre of the vehicle. This gave the carriage increased stability and allowed for an additional person on board. Thus the driver and attacker (wielding a spear, bow and arrows) were joined by a defensive unit who guarded them with a shield. In most battles, the chariotry likely headed the army and charged into enemy troops. The infantry, making up the vast majority of the troops, would then move in. Each foot soldier was armed with a sword and spear. Other weaponry attested to in visual sources included the battle axe and mace. Body armour was light and leather-based and included a plumed helmet with neck and cheek guards.

Soldiers were required to partake in oath rituals in which they swore loyalty to the Hittite king. These made use of analogic magic that counter-offered a curse for treachery. For example, one part of the soldier's oath used the metaphor of beer making:

> He [the ritual practitioner] places malt and beer seasoning in their [the soldiers'] hands and they lick it. He says to them as follows: 'Just as they mill this beer seasoning with a millstone and mix it with water and cook it and mash it, who transgresses these oaths and takes part in evil against the king, the

queen or against the princes or against the land of Hatti, may these oath deities seize him and in the same way may they mill his bones and in the same way may they heat him up and in the same way may they mash him. May he experience a horrible death.'[11]

The initiation also involved the soldier pouring a libation of wine on the ground, where it became analogous to blood: 'This is not wine; it is your blood. And as the Earth has swallowed it, so may the Earth in the same way swallow your blood if you betray your oath.'[12] Enacting these mock performances of symbolic penalties likely exploited the psyche of the soldiers, creating a tangible memory of the punishments that awaited those guilty of disloyalty. In our discussion of gender in Chapter Seven, we will return to another intriguing oath that threatened to effeminize those who disobeyed military orders.

Military campaigning was a source of revenue for the Hittites. Not only were valued spoils of war brought home following victory, but the campaigning secured access to supply routes and the future flow of tribute from conquered regions. However, military campaigns were themselves costly ventures that frequently put a strain on Hatti's economy. While there was a professionally trained full-time army (living in barracks and always at the ready), backup was drawn, when needed, from Hatti's already underpopulated society. Resources and manpower were frequently redirected from food production, and war captives (and probably Hatti's female population) were often used to fill the void in the agricultural workforce on the home front. Therefore, the expense of an ongoing military operation was avoided when possible. Mursili II reported an occasion where an appeal by the mother of a rebel allowed the king to abandon his siege of the enemy city:

I would certainly have marched against him [the disloyal vassal] and destroyed him utterly, but he sent forth his mother to meet me. She came and fell at my knees and spoke to me as follows: 'My lord, do not destroy us. Take us, my lord, into subjection.' And since a woman came to meet me and fell at my knees, I gave way to the woman and thereupon I did not march to the Seha River Land. And I took Manapa-Tarhunda and the Seha River Land into subjection.[13]

Underlying the merciful portrayal of the king was likely a strategic decision made for reasons of practicality.

A key feature of Hittite military policy was the use of treaties that were drawn up to keep conquered lands in check. By acknowledging Hittite authority in a province, treaties prevented the need for further military operations in that region. Hittite treaties most often stipulated an expectation for vassals to provide military assistance, information on happenings in the region and annual offerings of tribute. In return a vassal ruler was accorded the promise of Hittite military support, if needed, and was left largely autonomous in the administration of his kingdom. Treaties were renewed each time a new vassal ruler came to power in a subject territory. Hittite treaties are of particular interest to biblical scholars, as their structure bears a striking resemblance to the covenants between the Israelites and God in Exodus, Leviticus, Deuteronomy and the Book of Joshua. The common elements, in order, are as follows: a prologue that recalls the historical relationship between the two parties; terms of the agreement that specify both the obligations required of the vassal party and the responsibilities of the sovereign over his subordinate; storage of the document within a temple and arrangement for regular recitation of its text to the public; the summoning of witnesses; formulaic blessings upon those who uphold the contract and curses for those who break from the agreement.[14] This suggests the biblical authors modelled the treaties between God and his people on a form established by the Hittites. After all, the Hittites were most prolific devisers of treaties, with more than half of those found in the ancient Near East being composed in Hatti.

# FOUR

# MAJOR SITES OF THE HITTITES

I t is time to go on a tour to four of the most interesting Hittite archaeological sites. On this journey we will stop at the Hittite capital, its adjoining rock-cut sanctuary, a sacred spring and another important city known today as Alaca Höyük. They are just a few of the known sites of Hittite occupation, but they offer a great assemblage of visual and textual information about the civilization. Their weathered remains were once the setting for major episodes of Hittite history, as well as the daily practices and rituals of Hatti's people.

## Hattusa

The Hittite capital of Hattusa (modern Boğazköy in Turkey's Çorum Province) is now a UNESCO world heritage site. Visiting today requires some imagination, as only stone foundations remain of the great city walls and its buildings. We are somewhat assisted by the modern reconstruction of a segment of wall at the entrance to the archaeological site. This has been built of sundried mudbrick, made as an exercise in experimental archaeology that utilized a traditional Near Eastern technique. The form of these fortifications is based upon ceramic tower-shaped vessels found at Hattusa, which model the city walls.

There are five main occupation levels at the site. The first inhabitancy at Boğazköy was by the Hattians around the beginning of the second millennium BC. The second phase was the period of the Assyrian trading colonies, the city destroyed by

Modern reconstruction of walls at Hattusa.

Model of the walls found at Hattusa.

Anitta. The third and fourth levels are of most interest to us, being those occupied during the period of the Hittites. The third level of occupation at Hattusa, which was re-founded by Hattusili I, was destroyed at the beginning of the fourteenth century BC by Kaskan raiders. Very little was left following its sacking. The fourth phase represents the city that was rebuilt following the military campaigns of Suppiluliuma I, which drove the enemies out of the Hittite homeland. It was during this layer of the city's history that the Hittites reached their glorious heights. Even in the brief period when the capital was transferred to Tarhuntassa under Muwatalli, Hattusa was never completely abandoned. It wasn't until around 1200 BC that this level was deserted and then destroyed in flame. Following the fall of the Hittite Empire, a fifth layer documents a period of Phrygian occupation at the site, which followed the Bronze Age.

The Hittite period city started small, based around the high ridge of Büyükkale. It was here that Hattusili built the first Hittite palace. We have already noted the many strategic advantages of Hattusili I's choice of location: with access to an abundant supply of wood and water, and well positioned for communication across the Hittite realm, the area boasted natural defences, which were further enhanced by the construction of monumental walls. Postern tunnels allowed access in and out of the walls, while crenellated watchtowers provided a viewpoint for enemies approaching the city. Hattusa was not on a trade route, nor was it the locale of any major manufacturing activity for the empire. Rather, the capital seems to have served purely bureaucratic and religious functions. Much of the surviving decorative programme at the city is associated with Tudhaliya IV. The modern archaeological site is divided into two zones, with the southern area known as Upper City overlooking the older Lower City.

The most striking surviving features at Hattusa are a number of stone gateways that once contained bronze-sheathed wooden doors for access in and out of the capital. They are embellished with stone-carved figures. The western Lion Gate, which features two sculptured lions on either side of the portal, appears to have been the main entrance point to the city. Incised lines were used

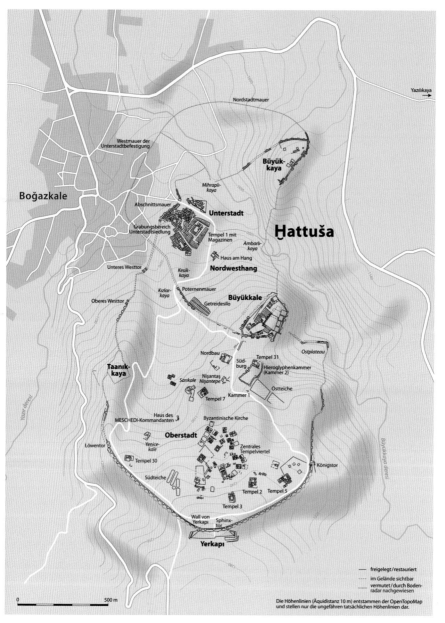

Plan of Hattusa. Like much Hittite excavation data, it is in German, the language of the archaeological teams who worked at the site. The Upper City (Oberstadt) in the south overlooks the older Lower City (Unterstadt) in the north. The Hittite palatial complex was upon the rocky ridge of Büyükkale.

Lion Gate at Hattusa.

to detail the wavy flowing manes of the heraldic beasts, each represented with its mouth open in a roar. There are two small depressions in front of each lion. These were possibly intended for pouring libations to the gateway guardians upon entering the city. Though the lions are heavily weathered today, one still gets a sense of their strength when passing between them.

The Sphinx Gate in the south is flanked by four sphinxes. Two of the stone beasts look inwards to the city; two face towards the outside world. They are female and wear the horned crown associated with divinity. The crown of one of the sphinxes sprouts a particularly ornamental antler-like motif that wraps around six rosettes. Each sphinx wears a 'nemes' headcloth in the style of the Egyptian goddess Hathor. Like the lions, their hollow eye sockets were once inlayed with stone. This gateway is atop a large rampart, and its elevation offers excellent views of the whole city. Stairs going up either side of the rampart provided access to the gateway. The Sphinx Gate has been described by archaeologists as being shrine-like, and it has been suggested the rampart functioned as the stage for ceremonial performances. Beneath the gate, passing

Sphinx Gate at Hattusa.

Corbelled tunnel through a rampart at Hattusa.

through the rampart, is a 71-metre-long (233 ft) corbelled tunnel known as Yerkapı.

To the east of the Upper City is the warrior god's gate (sometimes also called the King's Gate). On the city side of this gateway, facing inwards towards the portal leading out, is a stone relief of a warrior. His left hand is clenched in a fist, while his right hand holds a battle axe. At the waist of his belted kilt hangs a short, curved sword. The warrior's helmet has a long plume and cheek flaps. It also has horns carved into it – a horned headdress being a common Near Eastern motif for demarcating a figure as a god. He is both bare-footed and bare-chested. Great attention to detail has been paid to his incised locks of chest hair and even the cuticles of his fingernails. The high-relief figure is remarkable in its advancements towards realism, through its representation of the human body with its rounded features and depiction of musculature. It is likely this was the gate through which military campaigns departed Hattusa. The warrior god bids the troops farewell as they exit the city, saluting them in the hope of a victorious return. It is from this gateway that processions may have progressed towards the rock-cut sanctuary at Yazılıkaya, a kilometre northeast of the city.

The Sphinx Gate provided entrance to the main temple quarter in the Upper City. Twenty-five temples (of a total of 31 that have been hitherto identified in the city) were clustered in this southern area. These range from as small as 400 square metres (4,300 sq. ft) to 1,500 square metres (16,145 sq. ft) in size. They were roughly square or rectangular in plan. Each had the similar layout of an entry passage leading to a pillared courtyard, with the inner sanctuary located off-centre at the rear. Subsidiary rooms surrounded, and there was often a basement beneath the temple floor. Hittite temples (and other buildings) were constructed of mudbricks, with flat roofs made of timber and reeds plastered with mud. Only the stone foundations of these have survived. Some of the temples at Hattusa have yielded evidence that they were once decorated with coloured wall paintings.

Figure from the warrior-god's gate at Hattusa.

The largest and most important temple was the Great Temple of the Storm-god and Sun-goddess. It sprawled across some 20,000 square metres (215,280 sq. ft) of the Lower City. Dedicated to the two chief deities of the Hittite pantheon, two stone bases survive on which their cult statues once stood. Unlike the temples of some other ancient civilizations (whose sacred images of the divinity were concealed in a dark room within the temple), the inner chamber of the Hittite temple contained large windows that bathed their deities in light. These lost icons would have been crafted with wood coated in gold, silver and precious stone inlays. The statues were not affixed to the bases on which they sat in the temple – certain festivals required them to be portable, the sacred images paraded through the city on carts to multiple locations. A curious surviving remnant in the Great Temple is a cube-shaped block of nephrite. Whether this greenstone was part of the decorative programme (a statue base?) or had more of a ritualistic significance is unknown.

Greenstone in the Great Temple at Hattusa.

Besides the dwelling space of a deity, temples contained workrooms and storerooms for food and cultic equipment, as well as living quarters for the staff who attended to the deity. Daily food offerings were prepared in bakehouses, breweries and kitchens within the temple grounds. Textiles were manufactured in workshops to dress the cult statue or be worn by participants in ceremonies. Treasuries housed valuable objects dedicated to the gods, some of which were gifts from abroad or spoils of war brought back from campaigning. Scribal staff managed the temple's archives, which held clay tablets recording religious procedures and other official documents. In addition to the personnel operating in all these areas, watchmen guarded the temple from unauthorized entry. The open courtyard of the temple was the location for many of the religious rituals themselves. Sacrifices and the re-enactment of mythological stories occurred here. Musicians and dancers also participated in these various ceremonies, which will be further examined in Chapter Six.

The capital was responsible for the redistribution of grain throughout the Hittite homeland. Two subterranean storage areas have been identified, which were undoubtably a critical feature of the city, ensuring the preservation of this staple food supply. Eleven rectangular silos have been uncovered in the northern area now called Büyükkaya. Another 32 were located behind the postern wall of the Lower City. Both were used from the sixteenth century BC onwards. The underground granaries were designed to keep cereals at a constant low temperature and free of oxygen, prohibiting the growth of microorganisms and keeping the stock away from hungry vermin. This was essential for survival during the winter, as well as periods of instability such as a poor harvest or enemy invasion. That these should lie empty was much feared by the monarchs of the thirteenth century BC, who increasingly relied on imported grain (most of which came from Egypt).

One of the richest discoveries made from archaeological excavation at Hattusa are the thousands of clay cuneiform tablets from both the palace and temple archives. Some of these were penned in the Hittite language, in addition to seven other languages such as Akkadian. They include the aforementioned peace

Bronze tablet found beneath the Sphinx Gate at Hattusa.

treaty that followed the Battle of Qadesh, which was found in the Great Temple. Ritual texts are the most common type of document, giving us rich descriptions of religious life in the capital. A rather unique cuneiform tablet rendered in bronze was also uncovered at Hattusa. This treaty of Tudhaliya IV was deliberately buried beneath paving stones near the Sphinx Gate. Its contents refer to the division towards the end of empire brought about by a usurper named Kurunta. This rival dynasty was based around the city of Tarhuntassa (which, as previously explored, was set up and temporarily became the seat of Hittite power under Muwatalli II).

The palace of the Hittite monarch (located on the Büyükkale) is connected to the Upper City by two viaducts. Dignitaries would have arrived at Hattusa from the Lion Gate before making their way through this passage to the citadel, being there received in a rectangular pillared hall in which the king held audiences. The king would have emerged from the adjoining royal apartments to engage in diplomatic exchanges with the envoys. The hall was the setting for negotiating the terms of treaties as well as the receiving of gifts, tributes and correspondence from abroad. Much like Hittite temples, the palace contained a series of storage spaces, workshops and living areas for staff. In fact, residential spaces are yet to be found beyond those occupied by the palace and temple personnel. This makes estimating the population of the city very difficult. A large portion of the populace likely dwelled outside the city walls. Archaeological evidence indicates that the increased insecurity, apparent in the final days of the city, led some of these people to haphazardly relocate themselves within the walls. Some of the temples in the Upper City appear to have been repurposed as closely packed living spaces. That these people chose to adopt such makeshift dwellings reflects a loss of faith in the ability of the state to protect a peripheral population.[1]

Two late stone structures of Suppiluliuma II, the last king of the Hittite Empire, are located in the Upper City. The first, located on an outcrop of rock called Nişantepe, features the longest-known inscription in Luwian hieroglyphs. It has unfortunately been badly weathered and is mostly illegible. A few readable words of the eleven-line inscription indicate that the text summarized the military campaigns of Suppiluliuma II, including his naval battles against Cyprus. It has been suggested that the edifice may have been intended as a mortuary space for the king. Excavation at Nişantepe also yielded a huge cache of over 3,000 seal impressions. The second stone structure of Suppiluliuma II is a parabolic arch chamber that was once connected to a sacred pool.[2] Known today as the Südburg structure, it was once a ritual site, regarded as a symbolic entrance to the Hittite Underworld. Such passageways are referred to in Hittite texts as KASKAL.KUR. The vaulted walls narrow towards the back of the chamber where there is a relief of the Sun-god wearing a winged-disc crown. He faces left towards a depiction of Suppiluliuma II dressed as a warrior, with a bow in one hand and a spear in the other. Like the hieroglyphs at Nişantepe, the Luwian text on the walls speak of the achievements of the king. Perhaps in Hattusa's final days, these were attempts at propaganda by Suppiluliuma II, purporting that all was well in the Hittite Empire as it sped towards its mysterious demise.

## Yazılıkaya

Just over a kilometre northeast of Hattusa lies the sanctuary of Yazılıkaya. This natural outcrop of rock takes the form of two main chambers that are open to the sky. Each has been carved with a wealth of Hittite religious iconography. The site was used from the fifteenth century BC onwards, but it was not until the thirteenth century BC that the present reliefs were added. A gatehouse and temple in front of the site were also late additions. There are no clear references to the site in Hittite texts, and thus its ancient name remains unknown.

The decorative programme of Chamber A depicts a parade of 66 Hittite gods, many of whom are Hurrian imports. Some of the figures are identified by name in Luwian hieroglyphs; others by attributes they wear and hold; and others still are non-specific representations of divinity. Votive offerings may once have been placed upon the narrow benches beneath the figures. Two processions culminate in a central scene at the back of the chamber, approached by figures on either side. From the left advances a group of male divinities, while from the right comes a parade of goddesses. At the rear of the masculine deities is a group of twelve gods in the act of running. Swift movement is suggested by the overlapping of their arms and legs. Like the other figures in the scene, their godhood is apparent from the standard conical crown that each of them wears. Included in the procession of male gods are several mountain deities, their skirts rendered as mountainous peaks. The solar deity Istanus wears a winged sun-disc headdress,

Detail of the central scene of Chamber A at Yazılıkaya, where Teshub and Hebat meet.

beside a moon god who bears a lunar crescent in his crown. Two bull men, standing on a schematic representation of the Earth, hold up a symbol representing the sky. One deity has a seated bull atop his conical hat, identified by hieroglyphs as the 'Brother of the Storm-god'. The figure behind him holds a hieroglyphic symbol shaped like an ear of wheat and may be the agricultural god Kumarbi.

Interestingly the goddess Shauska/Ishtar, that great patron of Hattusili III, is depicted among the procession of male gods. She is rendered with masculine characteristics to emphasize her role as a warrior goddess. Her hair and crown are distinctively male. She wears a female skirt, but her front striding leg reveals that beneath it she is garbed in the short kilt typically worn by men. Like several of the male figures, wings sprout from her shoulders. Two (more typically female) divine attendants attend to her, named as Ninatta

Depiction of Tudhaliya IV in Chamber A.

and Kulitta. Their feet are concealed beneath their skirts, and they each hold what appears to be a mirror. The female divinities who approach from the right form a shorter procession. Each wears a cylindrical crown, some of which feature crenellations evocative of city walls. Among the goddesses are the patrons of childbirth and fate, as well as the queen of the Underworld.

The central scene, where the two parades converge, depicts the union of the two chief deities of the Hittite pantheon. The Storm-god greets his consort, the Sun-goddess of Arinna. They are identified by their Hurrian names, Teshub and Hebat. Teshub, like many of the other warrior gods depicted, holds a raised mace. He wears the conical crown of divinity and stands upon the bent shoulders of two mountain gods. Hebat faces him, standing upon a striding leopard. Her son Sharruma stands behind her, also upon a feline. He is followed by two attending goddesses, the daughters of Teshub and Hebat, positioned atop a double-headed eagle. Leaping towards the centre, two divine bulls emerge from behind Hebat and Teshub. Watching the procession of gods, on a wall directly opposite the central scene, is an image of Tudhaliya IV. The king is the only non-divine figure represented at Yazılıkaya, although his depiction here mimics that of the god Istanus. He wears a skullcap and a long priestly robe and holds a Luwian cartouche bearing his name.

Chamber B is smaller. The carvings are fewer and more dispersed across the rocky walls. Its entrance is guarded on either side by a pair of winged lion-headed demons. They have human bodies and raise their arms as if ready to pounce. Within the chamber, we once again find the image of Tudhaliya IV. This time he is accompanied by his patron deity, Sharruma, who towers over the king. The god wraps one arm around Tudhaliya and holds his wrist, protecting and guiding his mortal representative. Repeated is the image of twelve running gods from Chamber A, except here each figure holds a sickle-shaped sword. They have been interpreted as the twelve gods of the Underworld referred to in Hittite ritual text. A god depicted as an anthropomorphic sword on the wall opposite is understood to be another Underworld deity called Nergal. Several deep niches cut into the walls of the chamber probably once housed oil lamps, indicating its use as a venue for night-time rituals.

Though clearly a place of spiritual significance, the exact function of Yazılıkaya is still debated among scholars. It was most likely the setting for many religious ceremonies, including the preeminent Hittite New Year festival (known as Purulli)

Chamber B, Yazılıkaya. A sword-shaped god and King Tudhaliya ɪᴠ being embraced by Sharruma.

held in spring. Kings may possibly have been crowned here. The Underworld connotations suggest that Chamber B was used as a mortuary chapel in the late period of the empire. A statue base at the back of the chamber may have once displayed an additional image of Tudhaliya ɪᴠ, a venerated ancestral icon placed there after his death. At Yazılıkaya, representations of death appeared alongside symbols of fertility. In Chamber A the masculine storm convenes with the female Sun, a union that brings fecundity to the earth. In Chamber B, a sword-shaped god pierces the ground into the Underworld. Such contrasting imagery reflects the world view of an agrarian society dependent on cycles of death leading to new life.

A recent hypothesis by Rita Gautschy and Eberhard Zangger suggests the site had astronomical significance and was used for timekeeping.[3] They see the twelve lunar months reflected in the image of the twelve running gods. Individual days of the month (the stages of the waxing and waning Moon) were indicated by the

The twelve running gods in Chamber B.

procession of thirty male deities. The female procession reflected a division of years into eight- and nineteen-year-long cycles. Moveable markers could once have been fixed on the different figures to indicate the current date. Such a calendrical function does not dismiss but rather supports the use of the site for festivals throughout the year. Open to the sky, Yazılıkaya may also reflect an interest in the tracking of celestial movements. Even today, the natural light and shadows make the reliefs at Yazılıkaya become more or less visible depending on the season and the time of day. The relief of Tudhaliya IV, who watches the parading gods, is so aligned that it only catches the sunlight on several afternoons in mid-June (around the time of the summer solstice). At the conclusion of his sunbath, the king sits in shadow for two minutes. Another beam of light then dramatically emerges from a narrow gap in the rock to illuminate the cartouche bearing his name.

### Eflatun Pınar

Within Lake Beyşehir National Park, 85 kilometres (53 mi.) west of Konya, is a Hittite sacred spring. Known by the modern Turkish name of Eflatun Pınar, this shrine features a set of monumental sculptures carved on blocks of trachyte and installed in a pool of water. A 30 × 34-metre (100 × 112 ft) rectangular wall surrounds the pond, which was fed by an underground spring. The main monument is constructed of nineteen stone blocks and is about 7 metres (23 ft) in height. In the centre of the composition stands the Sun-goddess and Storm-god. Beneath are five mountain gods with their hands clasped together. The skirts they wear, bearing the form of mountain peaks, have holes through which the fountain discharged water. Ten genii figures flank the divine couple. They have their arms raised, as though supporting the three winged sun discs that top the monument. The renowned Hittite scholar Billie Jean Collins sees Eflatun Pınar as a representation of divine world order: 'Taken as a whole, the relief composition represents the cosmos, with the supreme deities of the land framed by symbols of the heavens (winged sun discs) and the earth (mountain gods).'[4]

The pool at Eflatun Pınar features other sculptures along its wall. Two small arch-shaped blocks, embedded in the wall on either side of the main monument, have each been sculpted with the image of a seated spring goddess. The wall opposite has another small representation of the Sun-goddess. A stone block below has been interpreted as an altar at her feet. The radiating solar headdress of the seated goddess is particularly well preserved. The torso of a sculpted figure was found in front of the altar – all that remains of her Storm-god counterpart, which once sat beside

The Hittite spring sanctuary of Eflatun Pınar.

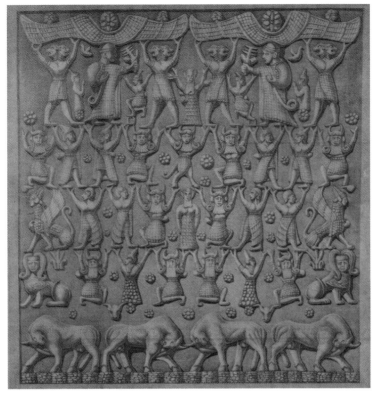

Ivory plaque from Megiddo, with Hittite iconography representing the cosmos.

her. On one of the side walls two divine figures are represented in movement, processing towards the main monument. It has been suggested that a gap in a corner of the wall was once filled by a huge block that was found nearby. It is carved with the form of three bull-head-shaped protomes. Holes bored through the block below the heads likely had a hydraulic function.

At Eflatun Pınar, architecture was used by the Hittites to manipulate and display the natural element of water for religious purposes. Functioning as an open-air sanctuary, the site was probably used for ritual cleansing. One Hittite text mentions a 'fountain of the Sun deity' that was used by the king for a purification and protection ritual.[5] Springs were also seen as channels for communication with the worlds below, providing a passage through which supernatural beings could travel to the human realm.

The Fasıllar monument. An upright replica stands outside Ankara's Museum of Anatolian Civilizations.

A healing ritual involving clay (which when retrieved from water was regarded to have procreative powers) retrieved from a spring contains the analogic incantation: 'Just as you, spring, keep gushing clay back up from the Netherworld, in the same manner remove the evil impurity from the body parts of this person, the patient.'[6] Interestingly, fragmentary animal sculptures have been discovered that were deliberately deposited within the pond at Eflatun Pınar. These were perhaps symbolically sacrificed here. Votive miniature ceramic vessels have also been found in the water – the remnants of rituals conducted next to the spring.

The decorative programme at Eflatun Pınar is comparable to the celestial scenes encountered on a small ivory plaque found at Megiddo. Now housed in Chicago's Oriental Institute, this object was likely manufactured in Hatti and came to the Levant as a diplomatic gift or as booty. It similarly depicts registers of divine beings standing atop each other. They include bull men, mountain gods and sphinxes. Their arms are stretched upwards, supporting each subsequent level of gods above. Double-headed creatures and two mirroring depictions of a king hold up winged sun discs at the top of the ivory. Four bulls stalk across a ground line at the bottom. Like Eflatun Pınar, the theme is cosmic order. Notable at Eflatun

Pınar, and on the plaque, is the fact that the divinities represented are front-facing figures. Illustration in profile is more typical in surviving Hittite reliefs. In the village of Fasıllar, 40 kilometres (25 mi.) from the spring, is an unfinished stone sculpture (also rendered frontally) which may have been intended for inclusion in the decorative programme at Eflatun Pınar. At a height of 8 metres (5 mi.) and carved in a single block of trachyte, it depicts the Storm-god standing on top of a mountain god. They are flanked on either side by lions. Today the monolith lies flat on the incline of a slope not far from where it was quarried, having never reached its intended destination. Weighing 70 tonnes, the task may have proved logistically too challenging for Hittite technology.

## Alaca Höyük

Alaca Höyük is a small site located 25 kilometres (15½ mi.) northeast of the Hittite capital. Hattian 'royal' tombs at the settlement

Pre-Hittite tomb at Alaca Höyük.

Sphinx Gate at Alaca Höyük.

date from the early Bronze Age, prior to Hittite occupation. Here, the dead were lavishly interred with gold and bronze objects, most notably the so-called Alaca Höyük standards. These cultic instruments of bronze, which bear the form of sun discs and animals, were likely used for the adorning of funerary wagons. During the later period of the Hittite Empire, Alaca Höyük seems to have become a major cult centre. No inscription has yet been found that identifies its ancient name, but the most likely candidate is Arinna, the city of the Sun-goddess. A dam dating from the thirteenth century BC at Alaca Höyük remains in use today by local villagers for irrigation. It is likely one of the ten dams referred to in Hittite records as being constructed by Tudhaliya IV. A fragmentary hieroglyphic stele discovered here indicates that the dam was dedicated to the Sun-goddess.

The main entrance into the Hittite city was through a gateway guarded on either side by a pair of stone sphinxes. They are female and wear necklaces decorated with rosettes. The main structure within the walls is a large building complex that has been dubbed the Temple Palace. It features rooms with evidence of cultic activity, as well as those that fulfilled administrative and redistributive functions. The Sphinx Gate at Alaca Höyük is flanked on either side by towers that display a series of sculptured friezes carved in low relief. The project of carving these reliefs of the thirteenth century BC was interrupted, as the sculptural programme was never completed. The orthostats are divided into two groups: those of a cultic nature and hunting scenes.

A festival procession is the subject of many of the orthostats. On one side it culminates in a scene depicting the Hittite king and queen worshipping the Storm-god in the form of a bull. The other side of the parade is directed towards the veneration of a seated female, probably intended to be the Sun-goddess. Many other human figures accompany the procession, some holding spears and/or musical instruments, or leading forth sacrificial animals. Most interesting are two dwarf figures performing acrobatics with a ladder beside a man with his arms raised as he inserts a dagger into his mouth. Dagger eaters are referred to in Hittite ritual texts – one festival involving six daggers being 'swallowed' in succession. Such a spectacle may be interpreted as a dance, performed while holding the point of the weapons between the teeth,

The original orthostats that lined walls of Alaca Höyük are now in the Museum of Anatolian Civilization. Casts have been installed on site in their place.

or perhaps projecting them forth from one's mouth. A parallel is found in a modern Turkish rural game that involves the thrusting and throwing of knives with participant's teeth.[7] At the rear of the procession is an incomplete carved depiction of an object on wheels. It bears the form of a large animal-headed libation vessel.

The hunting scenes from Alaca Höyük likely reference a symbolic hunt that preluded the depicted festival. It was the gods that controlled the natural world. The wild beasts who dwelled there were frequently cited as attributes used to define the powerful nature of divinity. Festivals that included a ritual hunt acknowledged their position and saw these animals be placed on the altars of the gods. An unfinished relief among the hunting scenes appears to depict this act, with a seated goddess receiving offerings of game from a worshipper. These orthostats also reflect the practice of collecting wild animals for the Hittite monarch's prerogative of hunting in the royal game park. The animals pursued in the hunting reliefs at Alaca Höyük are deer, lions and boars, and one orthostat also features a charging bull with its head lowered. These sculptures are some of the finest preserved examples of Hittite craftmanship. In our next chapter we will return to specific examples of reliefs from Alaca Höyük as we explore themes in Hittite art.

# FIVE

# ART AND MATERIAL CULTURE

ittite art drew inspiration from other ancient Near Eastern civilizations but added a distinctively Hittite flair to create something truly unique. Billie Jean Collins, writing on the eclectic nature of Hittite art, suggests that 'although the quality of the style of art showcased on the Hittite rock reliefs is difficult to defend when set beside the magnificent works of art from Egypt and Mesopotamia, it has the advantage, at least, of being original.'[1] In the previous chapter we saw many examples of art on a monumental scale, decorating architectural elements of several key Hittite sites. In this chapter we are going to continue to consider the objects that were created within the Hittite world, paying particular attention to their artistic qualities. These visual sources illustrate the distinguishing characteristics of Hittite culture. Now housed in the collections of Turkish institutions and other museums around the world, they provide information on materials that do not survive, such as Hittite clothing.

Hittite art reveals an understanding of civilized human existence in a world surrounded by untamed natural forces. Not only wild animals from outside the city, but the invisible forces of powerful gods and fantastical hybrid creatures are defined in art. Unlike some of the other great military powers of antiquity, the Hittite kings did not commission artistic depictions of their battles. Rather, the most common themes in Hittite art are religious. The images of royalty that survive are involved in cultic activities. Expansion of the empire coincided with the spread of this imagery. The reliefs of Hittite kings or gods carved on natural rocky

Hittite Old Kingdom stamp seal, carved in black hematite, and its impression. The design features the motif of a snarling lion above two recumbent bulls. A guilloché pattern surrounds the scene.

outcrops (that remain *in situ* today) functioned as visual markers of areas that came under Hittite control and influence.

### Art in miniature: seals and sealings

Seals are one of the distinctive traits of the surviving material culture utilized by civilizations across the ancient Near East. They were first developed by the Sumerians, alongside the creation of writing. As with cuneiform, they were much later adopted by the Hittites. Seals were both functional and symbolic. The miniature artforms expressed an individual's identity, being used as both a signature and to mark ownership. Stamp seals were simply pressed down to leave an impression on wet clay, while cylinder seals were rolled across. A cuneiform document could thus be signed by its author. Seals could also be used to secure doors or commodities within vessels. They were made from a variety of stones, semi-precious gems or metals. As with people, the gods had their own seals. In the mythic text the *Song of Ullikummi*, the gods borrow from a divine storehouse the sacred saw that separated heaven and Earth, before sealing the building again with their ancestral seal. The most common theme engraved on Hittite seals is images of the gods, notably those in which a worshipper approaches a deity. Scenes of the natural world are also frequent, illustrating

Tablet of Ini-Teshub.

alternating groups of animals with borders of vegetation. Seals may feature an inscription, identifying their owner in Luwian hieroglyphs and/or cuneiform.

Several examples of documents impressed with Hittite royal seals survive. A legal text in the Museum of Fine Arts, Boston, is stamped in the centre with the seal of Ini-Teshub, a Hittite prince of the thirteenth century BC. He ruled as the viceroy of Carchemish and was a great-grandson of the Great King Suppiluliuma I. The seal bears the image of a Hittite god holding a winged sphinx in his outstretched hand. Ini-Teshub is named on the seal both in cuneiform and in the Luwian hieroglyphic script. Another clay tablet,

Letter from the king of the Hittites to the king of Ugarit. Stamped with the seal of Tudhaliya IV.

in the Musée du Louvre, features an impression of the seal of the Hittite king Tudhaliya IV. It has been stamped on a letter addressed to the King of Ugarit that reviews the regulations on horses being used by messengers to travel between Hatti and Egypt. Rather than containing a pictorial motif, the central insignia of the seal is purely hieroglyphic. The king's name is flanked on either side by the hieroglyphics for 'Great King'. Above floats a winged sun disc, used to denote Hittite royalty.

The most notable surviving seal from the Hittite world is that of King Tarkasnawa. He was ruler of Mira, a vassal state of the Hittites. Tarkasnawa assisted Tudhaliya IV in military campaigns that suppressed insurrection in the west of the empire. He is the same thirteenth-century king represented in the Karabel relief (see Chapter One). The silver seal is now displayed in Baltimore's

Walters Art Museum. A bilingual inscription names Tarkasnawa in both cuneiform and Luwian hieroglyphs. This seal was in fact one of the sources that, in modern times, aided the deciphering of the hieroglyphic script. In the imagery of Hittite seals (and rock relief), apart from the figures with attributes that define them as gods, there are two popular recurring stock characters: an archer with a bow slung over his shoulder and an individual wearing a long robe. Tarkasnawa's seal is engraved with an image of the latter man-in-the-robe type. He wears a skullcap and his fringed mantle is open to reveal his forward-striding leg. Like other seals of this type, it is unclear whether the image is intended to portray Tarkasnawa himself or depict a god (his protector).

## Old Hittite polychrome relief ceramics

Hittite pottery varies widely in both form and quality. The vast majority is plain, with simple line decorations incised or painted on the surface. A group of relief-decorated Old Hittite vessels was found at the central Anatolian sites of Inandik, Bitik and Hüseyindede, and the pieces are truly exceptional in their depictions of visual narrative. Clay figures were sculptured separately and then applied in registers that encircle the vessels. The clothing of represented individuals is generally white, with human skin rendered in dark brown. The activities of the figures progressing around the vessels are rendered in profile.

The Inandik vase depicts fifty different people divided into four registers. The lowest register shows a banquet scene. Two prominent figures (likely a royal or divine couple) sit facing each other with a jar and table between them. One of the figures is gesturing towards the jar, while the other holds up a cup. Musicians accompany the festivities, including two figures playing a huge harp. Food is being retrieved from storerooms and also prepared by a kneeling figure. One attendant uses a stick to stir something within a large storage jar. The register above is interrupted at several points to make room for the vessel's four handles. It depicts a god seated before an altar, over which an attendant pours drink from a jug. More musicians, and individuals carrying ritual

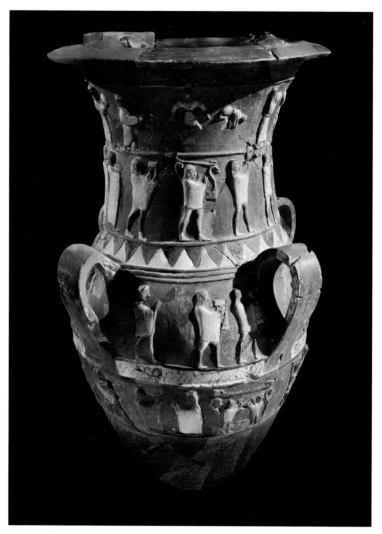

The Inandik vase, depicting a ritual procession divided into four registers.

paraphernalia, process towards a cult statue in the form of a bull, an icon of the Storm-god. The next tier depicts more musicians, being led by two individuals holding swords. They approach the model of a temple and an altar, behind which two figures sit on a bed. In the topmost register, the procession of musicians play-ing the lyre, lute and cymbals are joined by two acrobats/dancers. They progress to the right, towards a depiction of a sexual act – a man penetrating a bent-over figure from behind – that closes the scene. The inside of the rim of the vessel also features sculpted decoration in the form of four inward-facing bull-head protomes. A hollow clay tube connects these with a small rectangular basin. Fluid poured into this receptacle would flow through the tube and then stream out of the holes in the bulls' muzzles, flowing into the vessel proper. The effect must have been striking, a libation of wine resembling sacrificial blood as it spurted from the bulls' mouths. The Inandik vase depicts the rituals accompanying a marriage celebration, and was probably intended to be read from the bottom moving up the registers. The bride and groom may be a divine

Unveiling scene on a fragment of a Hittite polychrome vessel from Bitik.

couple, or perhaps the Hittite king and queen. The comparable Bitik vase is fragmentary but notable for illustrating an episode on the same theme: an unveiling scene. A male figure lifts the hood of a woman that sits across from him in a space that has been interpreted to be the bridal chamber.

Fragments of four different relief-decorated vessels have also been excavated from Hüseyindede. Two of these survive in incomplete condition. One of these depicts a deity with a lion, while the other has the kneeling-figure-preparing-food motif familiar from the Inandik vase. The other two are almost complete and have been fully reconstructed. Hüseyindede Vase A is similar in form to the Inandik vase, with scenes divided into four registers, four handles attached to the body and hollow inward-facing bull heads on the rim interior for libation use. It is also of the same size: 86 centimetres (34 in.) in height with a width of 50 centimetres (20 in.), which must have been a standard for this type of vessel. The four handles divide the two lowest registers, and the bottom register depicts a large bull in each of these divisions. The four animals are facing alternate directions and support the above scenes on their shoulder. Their heads are bent down, with horns poised as if to charge. Moving upwards, in three of the divisions of the next tier, an animal is being escorted towards the right. A roe deer, a red deer and a ram are being led as sacrificial victims towards the fourth scene of this register, in which a god sits before an altar. A musician plays a lyre, and a worshipper raises his hand in gesture towards the deity.

The third layer of Hüseyindede Vase A is the most interesting. A temple is represented, with its rows of mudbricks rendered in different colours. An altar sits in front of the shrine. A standard procession of musicians and worshippers, holding cult objects, approach the building from the left. To the right is a scene of two female figures sitting on a bed. A man stands in attendance, holding a bowl. One of the women is applying make-up or jewellery to the other, who is perhaps a queen or a goddess. It may even be that this is the statue of a goddess. Sculptures of deities are reported in Hittite texts to have been clothed, fed and paraded on vehicles in processions. The topmost register depicts such a procession,

Sculpted bull-heads facing into Hüseyindede Vase A.

Detail of Hüseyindede Vase A, illustrating scene of two females on a bed with a male attendant.

with an ox-drawn wagon carrying the attendant priestess and the queen/goddess to the accompaniment of music. The iconographic prominence of the bull suggests this vessel was probably used in cultic practice directed towards the Storm-god, with the female deity depicted being his consort, the Sun-goddess.

Hüseyindede Vase B is smaller, being 52 centimetres (20 in.) in height. It only has a single register of relief on the neck of the vessel.

Detail of Hüseyindede Vase B featuring scenes of bull-leaping.

The rounded body is plain. The main scene of the relief frieze is a depiction of three acrobats who leap and flip over the top of a bull. Normally associated with Bronze Age Crete, the 'bull leaping' featured in this illustration pre-dates the famed Minoan depictions from Knossos. It indicates a Near Eastern origin for the practice. Musicians with lutes and cymbals surround the Hüseyindede bull leapers. Two women are also portrayed, facing frontally: they wear long skirts and have their hands on their hips, probably engaged in dancing. While the Inandik, Bitik and Hüseyindede examples are the best preserved, sherds of polychrome relief pots have been found at Hattusa and a number of other sites. The vessels are amazingly sophisticated for their early date of the sixteenth century BC and were a precursor to the later development of Hittite rock relief. These ceramics are also unique in their depictions of humans, rather than the divine or royal figures that appear almost exclusively in later Hittite art.

## Illustrating the mortal and the divine

Few images of people in Hittite art fall outside the category of royalty or divinity. We have many images of rituals, but little in the way of representation of domestic life in Hatti or the everyday existence of potters, bakers or farmers. Our understanding of the military garb of the Hittites in fact comes from images of warrior gods. The frequency of scenes in which elite mortals meet with their divine benefactors prompts comparison as to how these two groups were represented visually.

Depiction of the naked body is rare in Hittite art. There are a few scattered exceptions in images of infants, and a notable representation of a nude goddess who holds her robe open upon the rock relief at İmamkulu. The Hittites represented their gods much like themselves, their divine status simply indicated by certain clothing. The Hittites used linen and wool for their garments, with belts made from leather. Men and male gods are commonly depicted dressed in a short-sleeved tunics that finish above the knees. Women and goddesses are usually shown wearing a long mantle. The major attribute that distinguishes gods from mortals is the wearing of a conical horned helmet. The more horns, the more important a deity. King Tudhaliya IV and his son Suppiluliuma II depicted themselves wearing horned headdresses bestowed with the status of divinity. Was this apotheosis or were these last two Hittite kings simply pictorially demonstrating their closeness to the gods? More commonly, a robed king is represented wearing a skullcap. Men tended to be clean shaven, with gods occasionally illustrated as being bearded. Size could also be used to indicate the distinction between god and mortal. In a relief at Yazılıkaya, Tudhaliya IV is being embraced by the much larger figure of his protector deity, Sharruma. Both humans and gods in Hittite art wear pointed shoes with a distinctive upward-curled toe. Several charming examples of Old Hittite pottery render the Hattian boot in the round as a ceramic vessel.

Jewellery adorned mortal and divine bodies of both genders, with hoop earrings commonly depicted in the ears of figures represented in reliefs. Archaeological discovery of such personal adornments has been rare. The people of Hattusa took their valued possessions with them when the capital was deserted and Hittite royal tombs, where one might expect to find such riches, await discovery. Though lacking provenance, Hittite jewellery survives in two notable small gold amulets dating from between

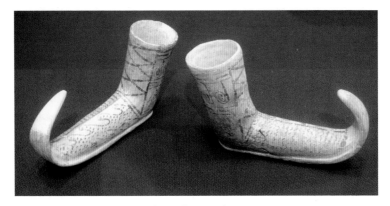

A pair of ceramic vessels in the form of Hattian boots.

the fourteenth and thirteenth centuries BC. One of these pendants depicts a male god, while the other represents a goddess. The female figure, in the collection of New York's Metropolitan Museum of Art, is seated upon a throne flanked with lion paws. She holds a naked child on her lap. The disc-shaped headdress she wears is likely a solar symbol, which suggests she may be the Sun-goddess of Arinna. The male pendant depicts a Hittite warrior deity, most probably the Storm-god. He wears the horned conical headdress and a short tunic, and holds a mace. There are two known near-identical examples of this amulet type, one in the British Museum and the other in the Musée du Louvre. A similar pendant in the Walters Art Museum, depicted in the frontispiece to this book, renders the god in silver. His arm is raised in a smiting position, although the weapon he once wielded has been lost. Both the male and female figures have a loop on their back, which enabled suspension from a necklace.

These small effigies of deities provide an insight into a key artform that does not survive: the sacred cult images revered as the earthly manifestations of the gods. Housed within temples, these large sculptures were made of wood overlaid with gold, silver and bronze. Ritual summoned a god's presence to come and dwell within the constructed body. The image could then provide a point of access to the represented deity. Cult inventories give descriptions of these lost figures:

Gold pendant in the form of a Hittite goddess with a child, *c.* 14th–13th century BC.

City of Lapana, divine image of Iyaya: One statuette made of wood, of a woman seated, veiled, of one cubit, its head inlaid with gold. The body and the throne are inlaid with lead. Two wooden wild sheep covered with lead, are seated under the goddess, to the right and left. One eagle inlaid with lead, two copper sceptres, two cups of bronze. Utensils of the goddess are present.[2]

The pendants evoke a cult statue in miniature.

Pendant in the form of a Hittite god, from the British Museum. A near-identical amulet is in the collection of Musée du Louvre (AO 9647).

Cult icons could be of human or animal form. As on the Inandik vase, a stone relief of the fourteenth century BC from Alaca Höyük depicts a cult image of the Storm-god in the form of a bull. The image sits atop a pedestal and is being approached by a Hittite king and queen, identifiable from their attire as well as the monarch's wielding of a staff curved at the bottom (known as a *kalmus* or *lituus*). Gods could also be represented as objects or as abstractions, such as in the form of a sun disc. At Yazılıkaya there is a depiction of a sword-shaped god. The hilt of the god is composed of a male head emerging between two lion-head protomes. Like other divine figures, the god wears a horned conical hat. Two further complete lion figures run downward along the shoulder of the sword. From their mouths emerges the blade. The tip is plunged into a line that marks the ground, the anthropomorphic weapon being an Underworld deity.

## The symbolic role of animals in literary and visual arts

Wild animals feature prominently in the arts of the Hittites, used to create images of the wild outside world of nature in contrast with the civilized society that existed within the city. The domestic animal is used in images of order and control. In a carved relief scene of a priest leading a goat and three rams to ritual sacrifice, the animals go willingly.[3] They know their place. The Šunaššura treaty describes the land of Hatti as a stable that protects its vassals, represented as livestock: 'Now the people of the land of Kizzuwatna are Hittite cattle and have chosen their stable. They freed themselves from the ruler of Hurri and turned to my Majesty.'[4] The domestic animal, much like vassal states, were better off for being under Hittite control. Certain wild animals were revered for their powerful or useful qualities, while others were used in metaphors for making negative statements about men. Hattusili I thus warns one of his vassals about defecting: 'Keep to the lion's side and don't take the side of the fox, who always does hostile things.'[5]

Visually, the deer/stag is the most frequently occurring and long-standing motif of Anatolian iconography. Notable are the

One of the bronze standards found at the Pre-Hittite tombs at Alaca Höyük. They feature the enduring imagery of deer, bulls and sun-discs that continued to be popular into the period of the Hittite Empire. This example, featuring a triad of deer, was the inspiration for the modern Hittite Sun Course Monument of Sıhhiye Square in Ankara.

early Bronze Age deer-shaped standards found in the pre-Hittite tombs at Alaca Höyük. In the Hittite period, the deer became commonly depicted being pursued by a hunter or mounted upon by a deity. A late Hittite rock relief, which remains *in situ* by the River Karasu, is one of many examples of this popular motif of the god-on-the-stag. A Hittite parable features the deer. The story begins with the animal being expelled from its mountain home and finding new habitation on another mountain. Here, it grows fat and eventually discontent. Rather ungratefully, the deer curses its new home. The mountain responds, countering the curse of the deer with its own: 'Why does the deer which I have fattened now curse me in return? Let the hunters bring down the deer! Let the fowlers capture him! Let hunters take its meat, and let fowlers take its hide.'[6] The underlining moral here is that one should respect the place they live and those that provide for them. Similar sentiment is found in a Hittite proverb that notes: 'When a bird takes refuge in its nest, the nest preserves its life.'[7]

Karasu relief depicting a god standing atop a stag.

Hittite king and queen before the cult statue of a god in the form of a bull.

In Hittite art, animals appear as the companions of gods, but they were also used to define the nature of gods' powers. Lions, for instance, frequently accompany representations of war deities. The depiction of a sacred animal by itself could also indicate the presence of their presiding deity.[8] The *KI.LAM* festival included a parade featuring the animals of the gods, rendered in precious metal. Gold and silver stags, a silver panther, a silver wolf, a golden lion, a lapis lazuli boar, a silver boar and a silver bear were included in this procession. Again, it is in cultic text that we find these rich descriptions of aspects of Hittite material culture which have not survived.

The sacred animals are often portrayed as being stood upon by their corresponding deity. The prerogative bulls of the Storm-god may alternatively be depicted pulling his chariot. On a relief at İmamkulu, his bull-drawn vehicle springs across the backs of three stooped mountain gods. Other animal–god associations are found in the literary arts, rather than visual representation. Ḫannaḫanna was associated with the bee in Hittite literature. The insect, with its notions of abundance, is most appropriate for a mother goddess who presides over the home. In a myth where the god Telipinu goes missing, Ḫannaḫanna sends a bee out to find him. She instructs the bee: 'When you find him, sting his hands and feet and make him stand up. Then take wax and wipe him off. Then purify him and make him holy again. Then conduct him back here to me.'⁹ In the *Song of Hedammu*, we find another rather charming example of animal imagery used to described Šauška (the Hurrio-Hittite name for Ishtar, the fertility and war goddess): 'Šauška anointed herself with fine perfumed oil. She adorned herself. And qualities that arouse love ran after her like puppies.'¹⁰

As with the gods, Hittite kings used animals to represent their royal prerogatives. Images of lions and eagles are closely associated with Hittite royalty. Recognizing their power, Hattusili I used both of these animals when describing the excellence of his person: 'his teeth are those of a lion, his eyes are those of an eagle, and he

Orthostat from Alaca Höyük depicting a lion hunt.

sees like an eagle.'[11] In his testament which stipulated the rules for succession, Hattusili I similarly used the lion as a metaphor for kingship: 'The god will install only a lion in the place of the lion.'[12] As we have seen, both Hattusa and Alaca Höyük featured lions and sphinxes (with their leonine features) as gateway guardians. These monumental stone beasts served to protect behind the city walls that they guarded from invaders or enemies of a spiritual nature. The lion is found elsewhere at Alaca Höyük, among the wealth of visual material carved in low relief upon blocks of basalt. In one such lively scene a lion is being hunted. A spearman approaches and thrusts his weapon towards the animal. Two hunting dogs surround and bark at the rearing beast, who attempts to grab the hunter's spear. The lion's head is turned to face the viewer frontally, contrasting with all the other figures of the orthostats, who are rendered in profile. Among the hunting group at Alaca Höyük is also a sculpture of a lion carved in the round, with its paws placed upon the much smaller figure of a crouching bull calf. The image of the bull being dominated by a lion was an enduring one, popular throughout the ancient Near East and even finding continuation in the classical world.

For Hittite royalty, the eagle was admired for its swiftness and acute eyesight. In rituals it acted as messenger between the mortal world and the divine. A religious rite for the longevity of the king and queen involved the use of a live eagle. The bird was waved over the royal couple while incantations were read. It was then released with the expectation that it would fly into the heavens and request long life from the gods. Another ceremony used an eagle's wing to summon the presence of the gods from their divine realm into the human sphere. Hittite royal iconography saw the production of a motif featuring the bird of prey rendered with two outward-facing heads. The symbol is found on small seals and monumental relief carvings, as at Yazılıkaya, where it is stood upon by two goddesses. A double-headed eagle is carved on the inside of the Sphinx Gate at Alaca Höyük, grasping prey (possibly rabbits) in each of its two claws. This motif was forgotten following the Bronze Age collapse but found re-emergence from the tenth century AD as a symbol of the imperial power of the Byzantine Empire. It has since been

Double-headed eagle beneath a gateway sphinx at Alaca Höyük.

adopted by a number of different states. Today this emblem of ancient Near Eastern origin is still used in the coats of arms of Albania, Serbia, Montenegro and Russia.

## Sculptural cups

The most elaborate group of Hittite art objects that survive antiquity are a series of sculptural silver cups, dating from between the fourteenth and the thirteenth centuries BC. These are directly referred to as *BIBRU* in texts. Zoomorphic vessels made of gold, silver, bronze, stone, lapis lazuli and wood are attested to in Hittite records. Some metal examples were made from melted-down booty brought back in military campaigns, then recast and rebranded with Hittite identities. Different animal shapes were associated with different gods.

The value assigned to these vessels is made apparent in a letter of Suppiluliuma I, which includes a silver stag-shaped drinking cup among a dispatchment of gifts to the pharaoh in Egypt. A silver vessel of such form is now in the Metropolitan Museum of Art. The stag wears a collar with a checkboard design, a pattern repeated on the lip of the cup. A relief depicting a religious ceremony wraps around the stag's body. The most prominent figure in the relief is a seated individual, interpreted to be a goddess. She wears a conical crown and holds a cup in one hand, an eagle in the other. The cross-legged stool on which she sits terminates in legs shaped like hooves. Two vertical downward-pointing spears stand behind the goddess. Not only do they form a border marking the end of the frieze, but they reflect the notion that, for the Hittites, spears were venerated objects and could demarcate sacred space. Before the goddess is an incense burner. A smaller god stands in front, atop the back of stag. He has a long plait of braided hair and holds a second bird of prey. His other hand bears a curved staff. This is Kurunta, the protector god of the wild.

Three worshipper figures approach the gods from the right. The first individual pours a libation from a jug before the deities. The second holds a loaf of bread. A third person is kneeling with a vase in his hand. A trussed stag beside a tree, with a quiver of

Silver vessel terminating in the forepart of a stag.

arrows and a bag floating above, concludes the right-hand side of the scene. It suggests that the three human individuals are emerging from a hunt and offering thanks to the divinities for success in their pursuit of game. The seated figure may herself be a goddess of hunting. Anatolian hieroglyphs, rendered in ovals of gold, probably identify the names of the two deities pictured. However, they have proven difficult to interpret and lack a definitive translation.

A second moulded silver vessel, also held by the Metropolitan Museum, is fashioned in the form of a bull. Bulls were the animal attribute of the Storm-god, being potent fertility symbols that produced thunder-like bellows. The stag and bull vessels are both

Silver vessel terminating in the forepart of a bull.

rendered in a kneeling position, with their forelegs tucked beneath their bodies. Both were made from several sheets of metal affixed together, the prominent horns/antlers being installed through perforations made in the head. A lot of attention has been put into rendering the musculature and veins of the animals to emphasize their strength. Inlays of shell or stone were once set in the cavities of the eyes, brows and nose.

A cup in the shape of a clenched fist, housed in the Museum of Fine Arts, Boston, should also be considered alongside this group. The form of the vessel reflects the practice of focused worship on specific body parts of the gods, each of which represented a certain divine trait to the Hittites. The hand was believed to be symbolic of the enactment of divine will. The wrist of the silver vessel is encircled with a relief. It illustrates a libation being poured before a deity to the accompaniment of a procession. The Storm-god stands

Detail of the relief that encircles the stag vessel.

before an altar while holding the reins of a bull in one hand and a mace in the other. He wears the horned conical headdress of divinity.

The procession approaches the god from the right, headed by an individual in a long robe. He pours the libation from a jug, towards the base of the altar. His dress and the downward-curved staff that he holds identify him as a Hittite ruler. A hieroglyphic caption in fact labels him as the 'Great King Tudhaliya'. A cup-bearer and a man holding bread are next. Three musicians follow, two bearing lyres and the third holding cymbals. A man holding a staff walks behind. The scene is closed by a horned figure who emerges from a foliage-covered mound – a vegetation or mountain god who looks on the scene. Floral and vegetal motifs decorate the empty space between the various figures, suggestive of a springtime festival.

Drinking vessel in the shape of a fist.

Twin set of bull-shaped vessels from Hattusa. The vessels possibly represent Serri (Day) and Hurri (Night), who pull the chariot of the Storm-god.

The cups have their origin in early Hittite terracotta zoomorphic vessels, notably those of the Old Assyrian trade colony at Kültepe. Many different shapes have emerged from excavations, including those in the form of lions, dogs, bulls, boars, eagles, deer, rams and rabbits. They may represent the whole body of an animal, or sometimes just the head. A pair of large early rhyta found at Hattusa both bear the form of a standing bull. Each has a ring that runs through the creature's nose. From these emerge the representation of reins, given the appearance of rope through incising. Each vessel has a raised circular vase opening on the back of the animal. The pair differ only in the direction of their tails. Found together, they may represent the two bulls (Day and Night) who pulled the Storm-god's chariot. Unlike this example, all three of the later surviving silver vessels unfortunately lack archaeological provenance. The themes of their iconography, however, are indicative of a religious context. Cuneiform documents recording temple inventories list sculptural vessels among the objects offered by the Hittite elite to deities. Here they would have played a role in rituals, used for the pouring of libations or ceremonial feasting.

A cultic phrase in Hittite records related to these vessels is the term *DINGIR eku-* ('to drink a god'). It is commonly encountered in ritual texts and is not exclusive to a single deity. Different gods are sometimes drunk in succession during a ritual. Does this simply refer to toasting one's drink towards a deity? Or was this perhaps more intriguingly a mystical rite involving human consumption of the divine? Were the cups themselves deified objects as other inanimate items were often viewed to be by the Hittites? Most convincingly, it has been argued by the Turkish archaeologist Yağmur Heffron that the phrase refers to drink dispensed from the cup of the god. It was a shared beverage, part of which was poured to the divine and the rest consumed by the human participants:

> They are partaking in the same drink as previously taken before the deity, arguably entering into a much closer relationship with the divine than would be possible through libation alone. Whereas a libation would establish a relationship of subservience between the human offerant and divine recipient, mutual drinking is effectively an act of sharing.[13]

There was an obsession in Hittite ritual with cleanliness and the need for purification. A surviving purification text concerns how these zoomorphic *BIBRU* cups must be cleaned. This would be especially important in the case of a shared cup that moves between the divine and human realm. They should be washed in a river, before being anointed with oil.[14] Anointing the body with oil following bathing was the same way humans may purify themselves. This also echoes the practice of consecrating the horns of animals with oil prior to their sacrifice before the gods.

Let us now meet some of those deities. In our next chapter, we will explore the various religious festivals, rituals and myths that accompanied the Hittite worship of the divine.

# SIX

# HITTITE RELIGION AND MYTHOLOGY

T he Hittites referred to their realm as a land of 'a thousand gods'. This was a reflection of their willingness to embrace deities of their neighbours as their own. Following conquest, statues of the enemy's gods were often transported back to Hatti where they were revered. After all, it was by divine permission of these local gods that the Hittites were allowed to take their territories. Persuading *every* god to stay in Hatti was also a means of preventing the divine sphere from assisting foreign powers. Occasionally we find attempts at the syncretism of overlapping deities but, for the most part, texts regarded each regional variant as a unique being. The Hittites were happy to recognize foreign weather gods as distinct entities, rather than as a version of their own Storm-god. Following conquest in Syria, the cult of the Storm-god of Aleppo was reduplicated and established as a sort of franchise in Hattusa.[1]

In addition to this adoption of foreign divinities, Hittite religion also preserves traces of pre-existing beliefs of the Hattians, the native predecessors who ruled Anatolia prior to the rise of the Hittites. Hittite religion was particularly influenced by the Hurrians. This is especially evident in a celebrated cycle of myths, which include the two texts known as *The Kingship in Heaven* and the *Song of Ullikummi*. They tell a Hittite version of a myth about the Hurrian agricultural god Kumarbi. The story begins with Alalu, a primordial deity who rules as the king of Heaven. His son, a sky god named Anu, makes war against him and overthrows his father. In turn, Anu's own son, Kumarbi, does the same.

During the conflict Kumarbi bites off and swallows Anu's genitals. This results in Kumarbi becoming pregnant with the Hurrian storm god, Teshub. In a bizarre dialogue, Anu speaks to the unborn Teshub advising him on the best exit point for birth from Kumarbi's body. Certain parts would defile the newborn's body, and he is thus advised to come forth from the 'good place'.[2] Teshub is born and, following the established pattern, contests his father's kingship. Kumarbi, unwilling to back down, plots against his son and travels to a great rock. 'His desire was aroused and he slept with the rock. His manhood flowed into her.'[3] This union leads to the birth of a giant made of diorite, who is named Ullikummi. Ullikummi initially defeats the storm god. However, by rallying the support of his fellow deities, Teshub ultimately prevails over the stone giant.

The story has been noted for its parallels to the creation myth told by Hesiod. This ancient Greek tradition also has gods overthrown in successions (Chaos, Ouranos, Kronos and Zeus) and features the motif of new gods springing forth from the castrated genitals of older ones. The bodies of male gods become impregnated with deities in both traditions, and the ultimate victory in the battle of successions is the storm god (Teshub/Zeus). The influence that Greece drew from Near Eastern myth is also evident in the Illuyanka tales. In this myth, Teshub fights a dragon named Illuyanka. He initially loses. Both his heart and his eyes are removed and kept by Illuyanka. To exact revenge, Teshub marries his son to the daughter of the dragon. Teshub asks his son to request the stolen body parts as a wedding gift. With eyes and heart restored, Teshub once again challenges Illuyanka and this time defeats the monster. Another version of the myth uses the ruse of a banquet set up by the gods, which puts Illuyanka in a drunken stupor and enables him to be overcome. The Hurrian storm god's clashes with Illuyanka resemble those of the Hellenic storm god's against the monster Typhon. Like Teshub, Zeus is initially defeated and has parts of his body (his sinews) taken from him by his serpentine adversary. These are restored, reviving the strength of the storm god and enabling him to vanquish the dragon.

Further similarities can be seen in the branch of the Kumarbi cycle known as the *Song of Silver*. It tells of a semi-divine figure who personifies silver. He is born of the union between a mortal woman and the god Kumarbi. Silver's peers tease him for growing up without a father. When his mother eventually reveals his true heritage, Silver goes on a quest to find his celestial father. The text only survives in fragments, but in one interesting episode Silver drags the Sun and Moon down from the sky. Despite his aggression, the Sun and Moon attempt to show Silver reverence by bowing before him. They plead: 'O Silver, our lord, do not strike/ kill us! We are the luminaries of Heaven and Earth. We are the torches of what lands you govern. If you strike/kill us, you will proceed to govern the dark lands personally.'[4] Following the pattern of his father, Silver temporarily usurps the kingship of heaven before being overthrown. His quest has parallels with that of later semi-divine Greek heroes, such as Bellerophon and Phaethon: both hubristically ride up to the heavens, but ultimately fall.

## Tales of gods in Hittite literature

A common motif in Hittite mythology is the search for the missing god. Their absence causes a disruption to world order. Only by finding the god, and appeasing them to return to their former position, can balance be restored. In one version of this, the disappearance of the Sun-god allows for the rise of Hahhimas, a personified frost. Without the warming rays of the Sun, the land becomes frozen. Another version, in which the agrarian god Telipinu vanishes, describes the instability that divine truancy causes:

> Mist seized the windows. Smoke seized the house. On the hearth the logs were stifled. On the altars the gods were stifled. In the fold the sheep were stifled. In the corral the cows were stifled. The sheep refused her lamb. The cow refused her calf. Telipinu went off and took away grain, the fertility of the herds, growth, plenty, and satiety into the wilderness . . . Barley and wheat no longer grew. Cows, sheep, and humans

no longer conceived, and those who were already pregnant did not give birth in this time. The mountains dried up. The trees dried up, so that buds did not come forth. The pastures dried up. The springs dried up. Famine appeared in the land. Humans and gods perished from hunger.[5]

The disappearance of this vegetation deity halts the fertility of humans, plants and animals. The gods go in search of him, and emergence from this winter is brought about by Telipinu's return. In another text, the return of the missing Storm-god allows for negative forces to be supplanted. Various evils such as disease, tears, fog, bloodshed and even a demon named Tarpi are sealed by the gods in a bronze cauldron with a lid of lead and deposited at the bottom of the sea.[6] Hittite myths are frequently embedded within larger ritual texts, whereby the myth serves to explain the purpose of the ritual. Stories of the missing god were retold and re-enacted as part of rituals designed to restore equilibrium to the world. Similarly, the above-mentioned overthrowal of Illuyanka served as a foundation story for the Hittite springtime Purulli festival. The triumph of the Storm-god (whose downpour gives life to the natural world) restores order, marked by the transition into spring.

Several Hittite stories revolve around divine interventions that disrupt the human world, reminding their audience of who was in charge. The myth of Kessi is about a hunter who is dominated by love for his beguiling wife. He is so caught up in his obsessive infatuations that he neglects to go out hunting. He is thus unable to perform his duties of providing food, both for his mother and as an offering to the gods. He eventually gives heed to his mother's pressure to take up his spear and head to the mountains in search of game. But it's too late. The gods, angry at being neglected, conceal the wild animals from him. Though he roams with his hunting dogs for three months, he finds nothing. He is plagued by hunger, thirst and illness but does not want to return to the city empty handed. Kessi then has a series of seven ominous dreams: he sees himself wearing a collar of wood around his neck; a boulder falls from the sky and crushes a servant; snakes and sphinxes appear

Neo-Hittite relief of a mythological theme, depicting the Storm-god slaying the dragon Illuyanka.

at his gate. The text breaks off at the point of the interpretation of these dreams, which probably held clues for allowing Kessi to restore the favour of the gods.

In the Zalpa legend, the queen of the city of Kaneš gives birth to thirty sons in a single year. 'What a horde is this which I have born,' she remarks.[7] Apparently disinterested in raising this small army of male infants, the queen places them in baskets and sets them afloat down a river. They eventually reach the city of Zalpa on the Black Sea, where they are reared by the gods to manhood. Meanwhile, back in Kaneš, the queen gives birth to another thirty children in a single pregnancy. They are all female this time, and she decides to keep them. When the thirty sons hear of this, they are convinced this must be their own extremely fertile mother. They journey to Kaneš in the hope of being reunited with her. The gods, however, have mischief planned. The mother and sons are made to not recognize each other. She therefore proposes marrying her thirty daughters to the thirty newly arrived young men. Only the youngest son opposes this, apparently immune to the fog of ignorance induced by the gods. He protests that such an incestuous union would not be right. The text is lost from this point, leaving us to wonder whether the taboo actually took place.

Two Hittite myths feature the motif of the childless couple granted offspring by the gods. *The Tale of the Sun-God, the Cow and the Fisherman* begins with the solar deity looking down from the sky. He sees a cow in a meadow and is filled with desire for her. Transforming himself into the form of a young man, he leaves the heavens and copulates with the animal. This results in the cow giving birth to a human child. The cow, confused as to why this child of hers has two legs rather than four, rejects the infant. She even attempts to eat it. The Sun-god comes down from the sky once more and takes the child, placing him in the path of a child-less fisherman. The fisherman is thankful for this blessing from the Sun-god and takes the baby home to his wife. He orders his wife to feign the noises of labour, so as to be heard by the people of the city. This mercurial instruction is aimed at extracting baby-shower gifts of beer, bread and fat from their neighbours. The second tablet, containing the next part of the story, is yet to be recovered.

The folklore trope of the wealthy but childless couple opens the myth of Appu and his sons, for though Appu has all the riches he could desire, he lacks an heir. He observes the elders sharing food and drink with their sons, but with no child of his own to share his bread with, Appu finds life lacking. It is suggested the couple's lack of progeny is a result of Appu's misunderstanding of sex, as he goes to lie with his wife fully clothed. Taking a lamb as sacrifice, Appu sets out to appeal to the Sun-god and discover what's amiss. The deity descends from the sky and appears to Appu, disguised as a young man. The Sun-god advises him to 'Go get drunk, go home, and have good sexual intercourse with your wife. The gods will give you one son.'[8] Appu follows suit and his wife subsequently becomes pregnant. She delivers a baby boy, and they name him Wrong. Falling pregnant again, the wife gives birth to a second son; he is named Right. Years pass and the brothers reach adulthood. Appu's estate is to be divided between them. Wrong, however, seems to get the better half. An altercation between the brothers follows and is taken to the divine court of the Sun-god in Sippar. The ruling in favour of Right is contended by Wrong, and the Sun-god refers the case to the goddess Šauška, queen of Nineveh. Once again, we are tantalized by a break in the text that obscures the story's conclusion.

Versions of the famed Mesopotamian myth the *Epic of Gilgamesh* have also been found at Hattusa. The epic tells of the exploits of Gilgamesh, a mythologized king who ruled the Sumerian city of Uruk in the third millennium BC. He goes on a series of adventures, from a journey to retrieve wood from the Cedar Forest to the subjugation of the rampant Bull of Heaven. The tale culminates in a futile quest for immortality. Fragments of the retellings found at Hattusa were written in the Hittite language, as well as in Akkadian and Hurrian. They seem to have mainly functioned as a scribal exercise, rather than a myth that was widely known. By copying down the adventures of Gilgamesh and his companion Enkidu, scribes learnt the nuances of the cuneiform languages. Interestingly though, some of these textual fragments were reworked to appeal to local tastes. While the standard Mesopotamian account has the hero born of semi-human semi-divine parentage, in the Hittite text Gilgamesh is not born but crafted by the gods: 'The great gods fashioned the frame of Gilgamesh. The Sun-god of Heaven lent him manliness. The Storm-god lent him heroic qualities. The great gods created Gilgamesh: His body was eleven cubits in height; his breast was nine spans in breadth; his beard was three cubits in length.'[9] Note the importance given here to the deities of sun and storm, chief gods of the Hittite pantheon. Several episodes are unique to the Hittite version of the Gilgamesh narrative. One involves an encounter that occurs between Gilgamesh and the moon god on the steppe. Gilgamesh has just slayed two lions. The lunar deity requests that Gilgamesh creates images of these beasts and offers them to his temple in the city. In another section, the Hittite Gilgamesh meets a personification of the sea. While the hero bows and blesses the body of water, he is met with curses in return.

## The role of the gods

In the previous chapter, we saw how gods were depicted in art. Let us now continue to explore their identities, nature and functions within Hittite society. As has been noted, the Hittite pantheon was accumulative and happily embraced the gods of neighbouring states. This god-collecting reflects a mentality of safeguarding the state from facing the displeasure of some forgotten deity. Indeed, in one prayer composed by Muwatalli, the king attempted to cover all bases by naming 140 different gods (many being regional variations of the Storm-god). Leading the pantheon of Hittite gods was the Storm-god and Sun-goddess of Arinna. Different names could be used for the pair, with the celestial couple assimilated and often referred to by the Hurrian names Teshub and Hebat (as at Yazılıkaya). The land essentially belonged to these two deities, who were responsible for maintaining its fertility. These gods were revered and feared, representing the uncontrollable forces on which human survival depended. The martial, thundering Storm-god watered the earth. The Sun-goddess was the source of light, whose warmth enabled life to grow. The king and queen acted as their human representatives on Earth. They themselves could become gods after death, revered as part of the ancestral cult.

Many other, lesser gods attended on various aspects of society. Ḫannaḫanna, for instance, was a wise mother goddess who was associated with creation and the hearth and was perceived to be present at the birth of a child. Inara was the divine huntress, the daughter of the Storm-god, who dwelled with the wild animals of the steppe. Hašamili was the god of metalworkers and craftsmen. Associated with smoke, Mursili II reported that, on one occasion, Hašamili cloaked the Hittite troops in the exhaust from his divine furnace and made them invisible to an enemy. The Hittites believed that their gods could play an active role in shaping events. Tradition held that the Storm-god accompanied the king onto the battlefield, for example. Such belief was no doubt strengthened by another report of Mursili's which claimed that one of the king's enemies was struck by lightning. Features of the natural world like rivers, mountains, clouds and the winds are cited as divine forces that acted as witnesses for treaties. Even in the everyday domestic sphere, gods abound. Inanimate objects in the home, like the hearth, door-bolt and windows, were personified with a divine presence. Deification provided a means of ordering and understanding the world in which people lived.

The Hittite king Tudhaliya IV being protectively embraced by the god Sharruma at Yazılıkaya.

Certain gods enjoyed periods of special privilege, being the personal deities of different kings. This elevated position was not, however, at the exclusion of other gods, who continued to receive appropriate reverence. The best example of this we have seen was Hattusili III's affiliation with Ishtar/Šauška, a relationship that essentially shaped the course of his life. The goddess is described by Hattusili as a mother-like figure, guiding her child by hand and guarding him from danger: 'The goddess, My Lady held me by the hand in every respect . . . Ishtar, My Lady, put my enemies and enviers at my mercy and I finished them off.'[10] Visually, the strong relationship between a king and his personal god is well illustrated in the relief at Yazılıkaya of Tudhaliya IV being embraced in a protective manner by the deity Sharruma.

Fruitful agriculture and military successes were signs of divine pleasure and approval of the Hittite state. But conversely, the gods could also be wrathful. Defeat on the battlefield and crop failure were forms of divine punishment regularly exacted on humankind. In the ancient Near East, the spoliation of a god's cult statue from a city by adversaries during military campaign was symbolic of divine abandonment. A prayer composed by King Arnuwanda I describes the plunder of Hittite temples by Kaskaean invaders and the subsequent neglect faced by the gods: 'In those lands no one any longer invokes your names, O gods. No one performs for you the rituals of the day, the month or the year. No one celebrates your festivals and ceremonies.'[11] Order has been inverted. The prayer concludes with a pledge that sacrificial offerings will be sent through enemy-occupied territory to the abducted deities. The symbiotic relationship between gods and mortals must always be maintained, which ensured divine protection for Hatti. Mursili II reports in a prayer on an occasion where the divine abandonment of humanity ultimately backfires on the gods, who would fail to receive their regular sacrifices: 'The plague does not subside at all, and they continue to die. Even those few makers of offering bread and libation pourers who still remain will die. Nobody will prepare for you offering bread and libation any longer.'[12] The monarch was considered responsible for any divine disfavour exacted on the state. Kings and queens composed prayers, like the above examples, in which they justified their actions, petitioned requests and communicated their feelings to the gods. The prayer became a vehicle of emotional release for Hittite royalty battling with the struggles of being human: 'Wherever I flow like water, I do not know my location. Like a boat, I do not know when I will arrive at land.'[13] Even with more than 3,000 years separating us from the Hittites, we can relate to such sentiment.

## Fate, death and the Underworld

Though various rituals were enacted to avoid predicted misfortune, the Hittite religion had the concept of a predetermined destiny ordained by the gods. Išduštaya and Papaya were described as Underworld goddesses who were '. . . spinning the years of the king. The shortness of the years, their calculation cannot be seen.'[14] It is they who discerned the length of a life. This same metaphor of life as a thread was to be adopted later by the classical world. The Moirai are well known as the three Fates of Greek mythology, who span, measured and cut off the lives of mortals.

The Hittites, however, had a second set of fate goddesses who coexisted alongside Išduštaya and Papaya. The Gulšeš personified fate itself. Their name is derived from the verb *gulš-*, meaning to carve, engrave, mark, inscribe or write.[15] Their prerogative was thus writing down the destiny of an individual from the moment of birth. It was the Gulšeš who were blamed for prematurely ending the marriage of the thirteenth-century BC Hittite prince Tattamaru: 'You, Tattamaru, had married the daughter of my sister, but then the Gulšeš treated you badly, and she died on you.'[16] The commercial metaphor of weighing lives as though merchandise was also sometimes used: 'Lo, I pick up a scale and put up for weighing the long years of Labarna; lo, I pick up a scale and put up for weighing the long years of Tawananna.'[17]

Lelwani was the queen of the Netherworld, who specifically determined when a person would die. It was to Lelwani that Puduhepa appealed for the granting of long life to both herself and her husband: 'If you, Lelwani my lady will intercede with the gods, if you will keep your servant Hattusili alive and grant him long years, months and days, then I will order to be made for Lelwani, my Lady, a silver statue of Hattusili, as tall as Hattusili, with his head, his hands and his feet in gold.'[18] Puduhepa also requested Lelwani to provide a cure for the king's 'fire of the feet', a condition thought perhaps to be gout or neuropathy. Temples of Lelwani were common repositories for storing treaties. This was perhaps in the hope that the goddess would bring death to those who broke their agreements.

Rivers were regarded as access points to the Hittite Netherworld. The riverbank was often the setting for rituals directed towards the gods of the Underworld. The water was used for purification, while clay retrieved from the riverbed could be employed in making figurines utilized in rituals. Clay tongues, for instance, were fashioned and then destroyed in attempts to negate the effects of evil spoken words that had cursed an individual. The gods of the Underworld could be summoned via a ceremony, in which a pit was dug by the riverside with a dagger. Over this, sacrificial animals were slaughtered. Libations were poured of wine, beer, honey and oil. In one ritual conducted on a riverbank, the practitioner speaks directly to the river and recounts the Hittite story of creation:

> When they took Heaven and Earth, the gods split up; the upper gods took Heaven, but the lower gods took Earth and the Netherworld. Everyone took its own. You, O river, took for yourself purification, life of progeny, and procreative power. Now, because someone says to someone else: it is terrible, then he goes back to you, O river, and to the Fate-goddesses and Mother-goddesses of the river bank, who create man.[19]

Following the tripartite division of the cosmos, humanity is created by the mother goddesses on the riverside. It is from the procreative clay of the river that humans are shaped. The river was both the place where man was created and his road of departure.

One fragmentary Hittite tablet describes a fearful soul as it reluctantly journeys towards the Underworld, going along 'the great road . . . the road that makes things disappear'.[20] The text notes that 'To the gods belongs the soul.' Death was the point in which creation returns to the creator. It was often referred to euphemistically as 'The day of one's mother'.[21] Sources on the nature of what lay after inevitable death are inconsistent, but for the majority of people, the Netherworld was understood to be an unpleasant wasteland. Parent and child are unable to recognize each other. Inhabitants dine on mud, and only dirty water is available to drink. The human condition is reflected upon in the *Prayer of Kanttuzzili*: 'Life is bound up with death and death is bound up with life. A human does not live forever. The days of his life are counted. Even if a human lived forever, and evil sickness of man were to be present, would it not be a grievance for him?'[22] This gloomy outlook on death was adopted from Mesopotamia and contrasts sharply with the optimism of the carefree afterlife of the Egyptians. Only the Hittite kings and queens seems to have received special treatment – the death of a monarch was described as the day on which they have 'become a god'.[23] A fourteen-day funeral ritual was conducted to ensure the successful transition of a king or queen's soul to this new state.

The royal funerary ritual is rich in symbolic gestures. The meaning behind these gestures is not explained, and thus much is lost on us. The text begins, 'When in Hattusa a great loss occurs, and either the king or queen becomes a god . . .'[24] Then follows a series of prescribed acts to be carried out, beginning on the first day with a plough ox being sacrificed at the head of the deceased. A jug of wine was poured as a libation and then smashed. A live goat was swung over the body of the dead king or queen. Food and drink were offered to the dead monarch, who was then cremated. The next day commenced with women extinguishing the pyre using jugs of beer and wine. Tongs made of silver were then used to collect the bones. They were placed in fine oil before being wrapped in cloth. This bundle was placed on a throne (if the king) or a stool (if the queen). A funeral banquet then took place; the participants toasting the deceased. A human figure, made from raisins, figs and olives, was constructed in the remains of the extinguished pyre. A pair of scales was displayed. On one side was placed gold, silver and precious stones; on the other was placed a piece of clay. The scales were then broken and held up to the Sun-god.

The royal bones were taken on the sixth day and placed in their final resting place, a bed within the 'stone house' (a tomb). A seated effigy of the dead king or queen was then created. From that point on, it represented the presence of the deceased. The sex of the figure was indicated with the traditional Hittite symbols of gender: the image of the departed king held the bow and arrow, symbols of masculinity; a deceased queen was given the feminine attributes of the distaff and spindle. The effigy was placed in a cart and chauffeured between locations used during the remaining days of the ritual. The focus of these rites seems to have been on transporting elements of civilization to the Netherworld for use by a king or queen in their exclusive afterlife. These included paraphernalia associated with farming, agriculture, wine production and hunting. Tools were broken or burned in these ceremonies. A segment of turf was cut out and sent down to the Underworld where it would become the king's bucolic dwelling place: 'This piece of meadow, O Sun-god, have it made rightly his! Let nobody deprive him of it, let nobody contest, and may oxen and sheep, horses and mules graze on this meadow for him.'[25]

Breaks in the text obscure several sections, including the activities of the fourteenth day. We therefore do not know how the royal funerary ritual was concluded. Many personnel, and more than a hundred animals, had roles to play over the fourteen-day event. Musicians and wailing women accompanied the sacrifices and incantations. Vast quantities of food and other objects were required for completing the rituals. The two-week-long set of prescribed mourning rites was an important mechanism that allowed the community to manage and maintain balance following the disturbance of world order which was brought about by the death of the gods' mortal representative. Once completed, a new ruler could safely assume office.

In death, a king was reunited with his ancestors. Old kings continued to be revered posthumously, their images placed in temples where they received regular sacrificial offerings. When the capital of Hattusa was shifted by Muwatalli II to Tarhuntassa, it was important that the ancestors were also transferred to the new locale. But even kings did not look forward to their exclusive fate, and appeals were made to the gods for its delay. One text has a dead king lament, 'Sun-god of Heaven, my lord, what have I done that you have taken from me my throne and given it to someone else? . . . You have summoned me to the ghosts of the dead.'[26] Likewise a fearful plea is found in the words of Hattusili I on his deathbed, to be held in the land of the living by the protective embrace of a woman named Hastayar.[27]

While the Hittite royal tombs are yet to be identified, several cemeteries containing the graves of ordinary citizens have been excavated. Osmankayasi, where more than two hundred burials have been discovered, is north of Hattusa. Inhumation and cremation (with the ashes stored in ceramic vessels) were both practised here. The accompanying grave goods are simple: shells, small pots and the animal bones of sacrificial rites or funerary banquets.

## Rituals and festivals

So how were the gods worshipped? As ritual texts are the most common document type to survive from the Hittite world, we have a lot to work with. While there are reoccurring elements, religious rituals were diverse, and there was no standard procedure. Rituals were used to address the everyday challenges faced by individuals living in Hatti, as well as those of major importance to the empire. State rituals could ensure the continued fertility of the earth or the successful outcome for an upcoming military campaign. Domestic rituals are largely concerned with health, prosperity and well-being. Temples were the usual setting, although many rituals were conducted outdoors. Rock formations and mountains, in particular, were regarded as sacred spaces in Hittite religion – places where the gods may dwell. As such, rocky outcrops were often carved into with the images of deities.

At the core of most rituals was a sacrificial offering. Sacrifice played a key role in placating the gods and requesting their support. Official sacrifices of the state cult occurred regularly to ensure the sustenance of the gods and to maintain positive human–divine

Rams are being led by a priest towards sacrifice in this relief from Alaca Höyük.

relations. Sheep, goats and cattle were the most common offerings. Sometimes wild game, such as deer, could be sacrificed to a god after a ritualized hunt. The chosen animal for a sacrifice was ritually purified, anointed and dedicated to a god. The animal had to be healthy, and some deities required their sacrifices to be a specific colour. A procession with accompanying musicians and singers led the animal to the temple, where it was ceremonially slaughtered. The meat was butchered and then cooked by the temple chefs into a stew. In one ritual text, a sort of sandwich was created for the Sun-god with the meat of the sacrifice: 'He/she breaks two loaves of ordinary bread and places them on the table. He/she places the liver upon it.'[28] Occasionally the meat was left raw, and certain organs could also be used for divination after dismemberment. The meal was then placed on the deity's altar.

This was the most important part of the sacrifice, whereby the food offering was transmitted to the recipient deity. The act symbolizes its consumption in the divine realm. The leftovers were then feasted upon by the human participants. This shared meal emphasized reciprocity in the relationship between gods and humankind.

In addition to the sacrificial animal, other foods were used as offerings in Hittite rituals. Libations of wine, beer, honey, milk and oil were offered as liquid sacrifices for the gods. Food was also used for 'evocation' (*mukeššar*). These rites summoned the gods to attend their rituals. Paths were scattered with various foods, to lure a god to a place of worship. Some sacrifices were burned and allowed to be entirely consumed by flame, rather than shared. The blood of the sacrificial animal was collected for other ritual uses. Bread could be dipped in blood and offered on the altar of a deity, or it could be mixed with fat into an offertory porridge. Blood, given its association with death, was frequently used in the rituals of Underworld deities. It was poured as a libation into pits, although one text also cites it being used for cleaning the new temple of a goddess. The temple walls, the cult statue of the deity and the ritual implements were made pure by being washed with blood.[29] Precious objects also made for suitable offerings to the gods and were secured in temple treasuries. A hymn to the Sun-goddess notes that 'the silver and gold in your temples is treated with reverence, and no one approaches it.'[30] Texts that list such temple inventories tantalize us with descriptions of such objects, which largely have not survived (or await discovery).

Festivals were a scheduled series of many rituals enacted over multiple days. These were costly events necessary for maintaining a rapport with the gods, but they also provided an opportunity for meal sharing. Sacrifice played a major role. In Hatti, each new month (determined by a new Moon) was initiated with the Month festival. Food was distributed among those who attended the event: 'They place an oily soup and they divide it . . . And beer for the palace, for all the members of the guard and for the whole assembly is divided.'[31] Over one hundred festivals were scheduled into the Hittite cultic calendar. The inauguration of the Thunder festival, however, was based on the rather unpredictable event of a thunderclap being heard in the palace. The assembly would then head outside and the celebrations would begin. Festivals were closely tied to the agricultural season in which they occurred, making ceremony of farming practices like the planting of the seed in spring and the autumn harvest. Symbolic acts and performances abounded. As part of the Purulli festival, an old hunting bag known as a *kurša* was exchanged for a new hunting bag, in order to herald in the New Year.

Dancing, singing and procession were common elements, although each festival had its own unique flair. The musical instruments of choice were the harp, lyre, drum, flute, horn and cymbals. Dramatic performances also sometimes accompanied a festival. Actors dressed up in animal skins to adopt such personas as lion men, leopard men, dog men, bear men and wolf men. One such performance involved chasing a leopard man out of the city and into the mountains. Another festival featured an act where 'the female archer shoots one time with an arrow at the bear man. She misses him, but she shoots a second time and pierces him. She shouts, "awaiya, ayaiya!"'[32] A temple official known as the ALAN.ZU has been identified by scholars as a jester, who performed bawdy acts as part of festivals. In one festival he bathed naked in beer; in another, hot coals were poured over his head. Some festivals were celebrated in the capital; others required the monarch to travel to different cities in the empire. One festival in honour of Hebat was celebrated in the city of Lawazantiya and involved a bizarre act in which the king bound up the cult statue of the goddess. He then demands a blessing of her, in exchange for releasing her divine body from bondage.

Bread was a common feature of rituals and festivals, both as an offering and in more symbolic gestures. One text notes the use of bread as a stopper, to plug the top of pits into which sacrifices had been placed.[33] Another curious example is found in a text that describes the *ḫaššumaš* festival.[34] Several banquets were attended by the crown prince over the course of this multi-day festival, which has been interpreted as a rite of passage that prepared a future king for inheriting the throne. Part of the *ḫaššumaš* involved the prince in food preparation, requiring him to grind grain with a hand-mill in front of the symbol of a vegetation deity. The rites culminated in a scene set at night-time, when the prince was made to lie down in a sanctuary. Loaves of bread were placed on either side of his head and his feet. A circle of beer was poured around him. Twelve cultic women were then brought in, but frustratingly the text breaks off at this climactic point. The symbolic use of food seems to refer to responsibilities that would be assumed by an upcoming king. It would become his duty to ensure the people (and the gods) of this agrarian society were fed.

## Ritualized sport

A feature of religious festivals enjoyed at the local level across the Hittite countryside was sporting matches; these included boxing, wrestling, shotput and weightlifting. A rather peculiar and uniquely Hittite sport is described in cuneiform texts alongside these typical athletic contests: cheese-fighting. *IŠTU GA.KIN.AG zaḫḫiyanzi* refers to fighting *with*, rather than *for*, cheese. This ritual combat was preceded by a number of steps, beginning with the pressing of the cheese. Following this, the cheese would be presented before images of the gods. After receiving divine blessing, it was then distributed to the people, and young men would engage in the 'cheese-fighting' game, in which the cheese was possibly used as either a combat weapon or like a ball passed between teams. It is unclear whether this involved a soft or hard cheese. In the case of the latter, one could do serious damage to an opponent!

A much later parallel from classical Greece has been noted. Xenophon describes a ritual contest from Sparta in which players tried to steal cheese from the altar of the goddess Arthemis Orthia.[35] Defenders guarded the cheese by capturing and beating the thieves. Michele Cammarosano, who has written extensively on the topic, notes that, 'Given the importance of milk products in the Hittite economy, the presence of a cheese-related game is hardly surprising.'[36] He suggests that at the conclusion of a battle, the cheese was probably eaten rather than discarded.

Aside from such regional athletic events, there are also references to official sporting tournaments held in the capital, which the king would attend as judge. These included equestrian games, archery and running, with prizes for the victors. In the case of competitive running, tunics were awarded to first and second place. There could also be humiliating penalties prescribed for poor performance. Those who missed a target in an archery contest were punished by being stripped naked and made to collect water.[37] Mock battles were also staged, notably that of the 'men of Hatti' against the 'men of Masa'. Hatti always had to win, of course. Those who adopted the persona of the men of Masa were given insubstantial weaponry made of reed – no match for the bronze armaments of the Hittites.[38]

## Divination

Oracles were a type of ritual that provided a channel to receive communication from the gods. They involved the use of various divination techniques to forecast what divine provenance had planned. It was a scientific art that enabled mortals to read signs placed in the natural world by the gods. Each portent had a specific positive or negative meaning. After receiving an insight into how a future event would transpire, a person could either change their plans or use ritual to divert an undesirable prediction. Questions were asked in succession to identify the cause of a problem until a positive response was received. Is the failed harvest the result of a breaking of an oath? No. Is the failed harvest the result of a murder? No. Much of the time, it involved pinpointing which deity had been offended and required appeasement. Divination was also used to discern an auspicious date for the holding of festivals or timing the inauguration of a new king. Mursili II made oracular enquiries to determine the cause of the plague that arrived in Hatti during the reign of his father, Suppiluliuma I. Although the sickness was transmitted from Egyptian captives brought back from campaigning, Mursili's oracle held Suppiluliuma's offence of murdering and usurping Tudhaliya III responsible for the epidemic.

Oracles could involve interpreting the movements of wild animals, notably the observation of birds in flight and the slithering of snakes. Extispicy was practised by the Hittites, in which the entrails of sacrificial animals were examined. The liver, in particular, was believed to have the potential to convey divine messages. Clay models of sheep's livers have been excavated at Hattusa, which were once consulted during these oracular enquiries. Inscriptions on their surface map out sections of the organ, which would have assisted a ritualist's interpretation of a freshly butchered liver. The size, position and markings on a liver all conveyed meaning. Oil was used for the Hittite divinatory practice of lecanomancy, in which the movements and patterns formed by pouring viscous liquid onto water were interpreted. This technique was the most affordable, probably favoured by the commoner who didn't have animals at his/her disposal to sacrifice in succession. Multiple oracular techniques could be adopted for an enquiry, in order to verify an answer.

A distinctly Hittite method of divination was the KIN oracle, which involved the use of tokens that represented individuals (such as an enemy, the king or the Storm-god) and concepts (such as desire or the prosperity of the land). Each token had a positive or negative value, and the result of the oracle was determined by which amount was greater. In an enquiry, a token was assigned either an 'active', 'passive' or 'receptive' role. The active tokens take the passive tokens and give them to the receptive tokens. An oracular enquiry of this method thus reads: 'His Majesty will go campaigning into the Haharwa mountains and will spend the night there. If we have nothing to fear regarding his person, let the oracle be favourable. The "gods" [an active token] stood up and took "fire" and "great sin" [passive tokens]. They were given to "the overseer" [a receptive token]. Result: Unfavourable.'[39] Just how the tokens were made to interact is a mystery. Were they thrown? Or drawn? It has been suggested that perhaps small animals were made to interact, each being assigned one of the token values representing the various qualities and personages.

Dreams had the potential to include potent messages from the gods. Omens could appear involuntarily while sleeping or could be actively sought after for an oracular enquiry. The Hittite prince Kantuzzili thus requested in prayer: 'Let my god speak to me in a dream . . . or let a diviner of the Sun-god tell it to me from a liver.'[40] Incubation, the practice of sleeping within temples, was employed for this purpose. The vivid description of a symbolic dream experienced by an unnamed Hittite queen was likely set down for the purpose of being analysed: 'Perhaps the horses would trample me. I, the Queen, seated myself on the ground and began to cry. The charioteers laughed at me, and then they led those horses away from me, so that none of them trampled on me or urinated on me.'[41] The meaning behind an ominous dream could conversely become the subject of an oracular enquiry. An interpretation of the dream was suggested, and the oracle verified whether this reading was correct. One divinatory text therefore states: 'Those bad dreams that he/she keeps on seeing and those signs of bad luck that keep on taking place, do they mean that you, gods, foresee defeat in battle during the Tanizila military campaign? If yes, let the oracle be unfavourable.'[42] In dreams, gods may express anger at transgressions or make requests for certain offerings. Warnings are given in dreams. One recorded nocturnal vision provided instruction on who to marry; another advised against travel to a certain place. Particularly unique to the Hittite royalty was the vow dream. In these dreams the sleeping king/queen encounters a deity and makes a deal, offering gifts in exchange for favours. Puduhepa dreamed of such an exchange between herself and the goddess Hebat of Uda, on one of the many occasions that her husband was unwell. In her dream the queen promised to give Hebat a gold statue and jewellery if the goddess kept Hattusili III alive and did not abandon him. Such bribery of divinity was also practised while awake, with the promise of gifts cited in many royal prayers. Dreams held particular importance to Hattusili III, who cited five nocturnal visions of his patron goddess, Šauška, in the autobiographical *Apology of Hattusili III*. He used dreams as evidence of divine support. They reinforced Hattusili's justification of kingship, which was necessary following the usurpation of his nephew Urhi-Teshub. When Hattusili was sickly as a child, Šauška sent his father a message in a dream: 'Hattusili's years are short; he doesn't have long to live. Hand him over to me so that he will be my priest and will live.'[43] Hattusili was spared an early death by the goddess, and thus destined for Hatti's throne. In another dream the goddess appeared before Puduhepa, promising continued support for the king during a revolt: 'I will march before your husband and all of Hattusa will go over to your husband's party. Since I have elevated him, I have never exposed him to an unfavourable trial or an evil deity.'[44] In dreams the royal couple enjoyed an exclusive relationship with Šauška, where they conversed directly with the divine.

## Ritual as remedy: pollution and the healing arts

For the Hittites, there was no distinction between medicine and magic for the healing of a sick or injured body: both were employed in healing. Societal problems were also regarded as a sort of sickness that afflicted a household or the state. The lack of distinction between the religious and the medical is a reflection of the Hittite understanding of why we suffer. Prominent Hittitologist Gary Beckman outlines this best:

> For the Hittites, sickness was not brought about by physical dysfunction or by viral or bacterial agents, and social tensions were not due solely to the conflict of egos desirous of incompatible ends. Most suffering was caused by the dislocation of an individual human or deity from his or her proper position in the cosmos. Such dislocation resulted in a corresponding inability to perform one's role within the universe, with proportional consequences for others within the social nexus.[45]

The aforementioned dislocation may be the result of divine anger directed at an individual. This could be ascertained through oracles, so that the appropriate deity could then be placated. Or perhaps they were the victim of ritual pollution (known as *papratar*), which resulted from illicit human behaviour. A transgression, be it deliberate or accidental, branded an individual with impurity. It could then spread and affect the wider community. Murder, theft and other taboos were prime causes, as well as simply stumbling upon a polluted object. The incorrect disposal of waste from a purification ritual, for instance, could infect others with the washed-off evil. Pollution could be inherited and passed down for generations. Women in particular required ritual cleansing, as birth and menstruation were considered spreaders of pollution. Following sex, washing was imperative. Many healing rituals countered sorcery, which was also considered a major cause of illness. Mursili II banished his stepmother for this offence, accusing her of causing the sickness and death of his beloved wife, Gassulawiya.

Female practitioners known as 'Wise Women' (ḫašauwa) provided ritual means that offered a cure for illnesses and atonement from pollution. The remedial rituals they conducted made strong use of analogic magic. This called on the qualities of various plants, animals, people, gods and items which would become symbolic metaphors that could counter negative afflictions. Brushwood was set alight to burn up excessive anger. A fertile cow offered fertility to a barren woman. As a river carries away ships, so too can it carry away evil. Ailments were given a tangible form in figurines, which pain could be transferred to, and then destroyed. Wax was an especially potent substance for this sort of purification. Its protective association was apparent from its use for the sealing of contents inside vessels. Evils could be rendered physically in wax, before being melted away to the accompaniment of verbal incantation. We will look further at the profession of ḫašauwa in the next chapter, when we consider the roles of women in society.

There was a Hittite obsession with maintaining physical hygiene as a safeguard against spiritual impurity. Bathing played an important role in the cleansing rituals performed: 'As water is pure . . . so may the sacrificer Taduhepa be pure before gods and men.'[46] The water used for purification may be ritually prepared first. Night-time exposure had the potential to consecrate and purify substances, and thus several ritual texts from Kizzuwatna reference the practice of leaving vessels of water to 'spend the night under the stars'.[47] Cultic activity relied on access to springs like that of Eflatun Pınar, a site which attests to the reverence given to the liquid element.

While pigs and dogs were regarded as unclean animals, they were, rather paradoxically, used frequently in purification rituals. A puppy might be waved over a patient or placed upon various body parts to absorb evil afflicting him/her.[48] In one unsettling ritual, a puppy was cut in half. The bisected animal was then positioned on either side of a gateway, and evil affliction was absorbed into its body as a person passed through. Dog faeces was also used in purification. The excrement was mixed with dough and formed into figurines that represented demons. By knocking the poo demon off the shoulder of an afflicted individual, pollution was expelled from their body.[49] Both the animals and other equipment used in purification rites were cut up and disposed of, either through burning or burying, upon completion of the ritual.

There were also physicians who treated illnesses through the administration of drugs, the prescription of certain foods and the application of poultices. Common complaints they faced included impotence, wounds and eye problems, as well as respiratory and intestinal diseases. The role of the physician was fluid – they are referred to in texts as also playing key roles in various religious rites. In one ritual for the god Telipinu, a physician was required to sing while playing a musical instrument. He then performed a dance that included acts of self-mutilation. The roles of the ritualist and the physician complemented and overlapped each other. At the heart of any treatment, divine will was necessary for the ailment to be cured.

Pollution could also affect divine beings. It was therefore essential their mortal attendants maintained impeccable hygiene. In a text known as the *Instructions to Temple Officials*, the following was prescribed for those who fed and clothed the gods:

> Those who prepare the daily loaves must be clean. They must be bathed and groomed, and their hair and nails removed. They must be clothed in clean garments. They must not prepare the loaves while in an unclean state. The bakery where the loaves are baked must be swept and scrubbed. Further, no pig or dog is permitted at the door of the place where the loaves are broken.[50]

An attendant who served a deity with food from an unclean container was punished, by being force-fed faeces and urine. A steward of the gods who neglected to bathe after sex faced the death penalty. Cleanliness was likewise an expectation for those who attended on the king. In the *Instructions for Palace Personnel to Ensure the King's Purity*, a monarch beseeches the Sun god: 'Whoever does something in an unclean way and offers to the king polluted water, pour you, O gods, that man's soul out like water!'[51] Water served to the king was to be strained first. This Hittite document cites an example where this failed to occur and a hair was discovered in the royal water pitcher. The furious king ordered death for the individual found guilty of causing this contamination.

### Ritual substitution and scapegoats

The well-being of society depended on the well-being of Hatti's king. If divination ascertained that the king's life was threatened, a ritual saw the replacement of the monarch with a substitute. In the substitute-king ritual, a prisoner of war was temporarily placed on the throne in lieu of the real king. The stand-in was anointed with the oil of kingship while an incantation was read: 'Behold, this one is the king. I have bestowed the name of kingship upon this one. I have clothed this one in the garments of kingship, and I have put the cap of kingship on this one. Evil omen, short years, short days take note of this man and go after this substitute.'[52] He was then returned to the enemy homeland, taking the evil with him. Afterwards, the real king could safely return to the throne. The practice had its origins in Mesopotamia, although there the substitute king was executed at the end of the ritual. Animals were also commonly used as substitutes in a number of Hittite rituals. Both live animals and clay models were used in rites designed to redirect a physical affliction or evil presence from a person to a scapegoat. Words of incantation could transfer the ailment, as could touching the animal or having it waved over the victim. In one substitution ritual, people spat into the mouth of a black sheep who, having received their maladies, was sacrificed. Birds, donkeys, goats, oxen, sheep, dogs and pigs were the animals of choice for substitution. Even a mouse could function as a scapegoat, a ritual from Kizzuwatna prescribing that

She wraps a small piece of tin in a bowstring. She wraps it around the offerant's right hand and foot. Then she takes it away from them and she transfers it to the mouse and she says, 'I have taken away the evil from you and transferred it to the mouse, now let this mouse take it to the high mountains, the deep valleys, the long roads.'[53]

More obscure still is an instance of a fish being used as the substitute: it was flapped over a patient in the hope of swimming an affliction out to sea.

The most noteworthy documentation of a Hittite substitution ritual enacted was by Mursili II. The king had suffered from a sudden loss of speech, which occurred after the traumatic experience of driving his chariot through a thunderstorm. He re-experienced the event in a number of dreams, including one in which a god placed his hand over Mursili's mouth. The king's affliction was probably the result of a stroke. An ox was chosen and adorned as his substitute. Mursili was made to lay his hand upon the animal, which was then sent to the temple of the Storm-god in Kummanni. A wagonload of the king's possessions was sent along with the ox, including the chariot and the garments he was wearing on the day he was struck with the impairment. Both the animal and these items were to be burned as an offering to the Storm-god on their arrival. A second ox was also sent with the dispatch to Kummanni. In the event that the first ox died on the way, it would function as a substitute for the substitute. It is unknown whether Mursili ever recovered from his speech paralysis.

# SEVEN

# SOCIETY AND THE LAW

A discussion on society in the Hittite world is best introduced with an examination of Hittite law. Much of what we know about the daily life of ordinary people is preserved in the two hundred clauses of the Hittite laws. Our understanding of Hittite society largely revolves around the elite. The laws are unique among other surviving epigraphic sources, in that we get glimpses into aspects of the lives and treatment of the lower classes. Each law follows the pattern that if $x$ occurs, then $y$ is the consequence: 'If someone injures a person and makes him ill, he shall provide medical care for him. In his place, he shall provide a person to work his estate while he recovers. When he recovers, the assailant will give him six shekels of silver, and will also pay the doctor's fee.'[1]

Like the famous Babylonian law code of Hammurabi, these laws were intended as guidelines rather than fixed sentences. In fact, the Hittites gave preference to the pre-existing local laws of their subject territories when in discrepancy with the Hittite laws. However, the Hittite laws differed from the earlier Babylonian laws in their emphasis on compensation rather than retributive justice. The *lex talionis* principle of Hammurabi's law code saw that if a man broke the bones of another man (of equal status), he in turn would have his bones broken; the Hittite laws favoured payment. Hammurabi's law code began with a preamble claiming divine inspiration from the Mesopotamian sun god Shamash. The Hittite document, by contrast, was presented as a straight-to-the-point and secular set of laws.

There was a strong emphasis in the laws on the protection of property. This extended to protection of merchants, with more severe penalties imposed on those who stole the goods of traders. After all, without merchants, Hatti would lose access to luxury goods not available or produced in the heart of the empire. The Hittite economy was agriculture-based. Theft or damage to crops or livestock was therefore also of key concern in the laws. The Hittite laws have an aversion to the use of the death penalty for crimes, a reflection of the constant lack of manpower faced throughout Hatti's history. Exile was generally used instead, although capital punishment was frequently prescribed for some crimes of a sexual nature. Blinding was the common penalty for those who broke oaths, or for rebel leaders. Like Samson of the Bible, the blinded criminal was then likely to have been put to work in the millhouse.

Trials were held at the city gates. Legal transcripts indicate that each party swore an oath and then gave their testimony. On occasions when reaching a verdict proved difficult, the river ordeal (or sometimes trial upon 'the wheel') was used to prove an individual's guilt or innocence. Great importance was placed on impartiality for all: 'Do not make the better case worse or the worse case better. Do what is just.'[2] While justice was dispensed locally by governors, the king was the supreme legal power. A key principle of Hittite law was that anyone who lived within the empire had the right of appeal to the king against a judgement given at a regional level.

## Employment, agriculture and food production

Occupations in Hatti were generally inherited, with trades being passed from father to son. Sometimes a family may have been in the position to pay a craftsman to employ their son as an apprentice. One of the laws relates that additional payment was required if a son reached the point of mastery under the craftsman's guidance: 'If anyone gives his son for training either as a carpenter or a smith, a weaver, a leather-worker or a fuller, he shall pay 6 shekels as the fee for the training. If the teacher makes the student an expert, the student's parent shall give to the teacher one person.'[3] Craftsmen could operate independently, or find employment among the personnel of temples or the palace. Some positions were by royal appointment. It was the agricultural industry, however, that provided the livelihood for the vast majority of people.

Farmland could be owned, leased or allocated to be worked on by an individual or family. Rather than functioning as a single large estate, farms were spread as small parcels of land over multiple locations. The household of a typical farming family is recorded in the inventory of a certain Tiwatapara, who lived with his wife, Azzia, and their three children. The family lived on one plot of land with the majority of their livestock. Tiwatapara's oxen grazed on an additional acre of meadow in another town called Parkalla. A further 1.4 hectares (3.5 ac) of land in a place called Hanzusra were used for a vineyard, as well as an orchard of 40 apple trees and 42 pomegranate trees. The Hittite economy relied on this system of farming diverse produce over small scattered plots to fully exploit the agrarian potential of the land.

Different types of grain were farmed, including emmer, einkorn and *Triticum aestivum* wheat as well as barley. Vegetables grown included cucumbers, carrots, onions, garlic, leeks and lettuces. Legumes were widely enjoyed, such as peas, beans, lentils and chickpeas. Nuts and seeds are sometimes mentioned in Hittite texts, including pistachios, almonds, sesame and linseed. Parsley, cumin and coriander are among the herbs used in Hittite cooking. Of fruit, we have references to apples, figs, pomegranates, pears and apricots. Grapes were grown, enjoyed both in dried form as raisins (a common ration taken on military campaigns) and used in viticulture. The Hittite word for wine was *wiyana*, and several different varieties are referred to in texts, including 'red wine', 'honeyed wine', 'sweet wine', 'sour wine', 'good wine', 'pure wine' and 'new wine'.[4] Wine was a symbol of high status, its value attested at court as a prize: 'When they hold a shooting match before the king, whoever scores a hit, to him they give wine to drink.'[5] Outside a few scant references to its consumption among the elite, the majority of wine drinking occurred in a ritual context.

Olives were grown for their oil and to be used in Hittite cooking, as well as ubiquitously in ritual for various acts of anointing and offering. There are references to olive oil being enjoyed with dipped bread. One document tells the story of a dog who seizes a freshly baked loaf from the oven. The connoisseur hound dips the bread in olive oil before gobbling it up.[6] In an incantation text, comparison is drawn between the olive which holds oil in its heart, the grape which holds wine in its heart, and the god who holds goodness in his heart towards the land of Hatti.[7] Oil is listed as one of life's elementary needs in another Old Hittite text concerning compassion for the poor: the hungry should be given food, the thirsty should be given water, the naked are to be clothed and oil is to be provided for those who are dried out.[8]

Records note the keeping of bees for honey and wax. A sweet pastry known as NINDA.Ì.E.DÉ.A was made from baking a mixture of honey and flour with either sheep fat, butter or oil.[9] It finds modern echoes in the traditional Turkish sweet called *un helvası*. Sheep, goats, pigs, donkeys, horses, cattle and poultry were kept as livestock. In addition to food, animals produced wool and leather, and functioned as beasts of burden. Interestingly there are no references to the consumption of eggs, although several types of poultry were eaten. Most Hittite cooking seems to have taken the form of soups and stews. Meat would have been too expensive to be eaten on a regular basis for all but the wealthy. To prevent spoilage of excess meat, or to delay its consumption, it was often preserved by being dried out. Dairy formed a fundamental part of the Hittite diet. Butter and cheese were employed in cooking – both are cited as ingredients used in baking various types of breads. While by this time hunting was no longer a major source of food procurement, it still had a symbolic role and was enjoyed as a sport of the elite. Archaeological excavations from Hittite urban centres have yielded the bones of a range of wild animals including a badger, weasel, deer, boar, bear, lion, leopard, hare, tortoise, molluscs and different types of fish (even a shark).[10]

## Kingship and the king's officials

The kings of Hatti played a major role in religious life, acting as the gods' representatives in the role of high priest. A king was divinely appointed. It was the gods who owned the land, and the monarch was simply the custodian: 'May the Labarna, the king, be dear to the gods! The land belongs to the Storm-god alone. Heaven, Earth, and the people belong to the Storm-god alone. He has made the Labarna, the king, his administrator and given him the entire land of Hatti.'[11] Maintaining relations between the human and divine realms was an essential function of kingship that assured societal success. In the plague prayers of Mursili II, we saw how a king was held accountable when divine displeasure afflicted the land, and it became his responsibility to provide remedy. Although not considered gods while living, former kings were deified and received offerings. The king was a conduit to the gods in life and became part of their divine realm in death.

The other key prerogative of kingship was the expansion of Hatti's borders through military conquest: a king's ability on the battleground determined his fitness to rule. The king was also the head of the judicial system and passed verdict on the most serious legal cases in Hatti. He represented the country on the world stage, forging treaties and sending letters to maintain diplomatic relations with foreign powers. But for the majority of people living within Hatti's borders he was a far, remote figure – someone who you might get a fleeting glimpse of at a festival. The Hittite king Hattusili I, who set the paradigm for kingship, wrote, 'Let no one think, "In secret the king does what he pleases saying, 'I can justify it, whether it is right, or whether it is not right'".'[12] The king, therefore, relied on the judgement and assistance of others in administrating the empire. These included high-ranking scribes, priests and military commanders. The royal guard were charged with protecting the king's person while he was campaigning abroad or attending festivals. Another group known as the 'men of the golden spear' provided security at home in the palatial precinct.

At Hattusa, the chief civic official appointed by the king was known as the *Hazannu* (often translated as 'mayor'). The civic matters he managed included security, water access, sanitation and fire protection. Fire was understandably much feared for a civilization whose buildings were mostly timber and mudbrick. The destruction of a public building by flame is given by Puduhepa as the reason for the delays in sending Ramesses a Hittite princess.

It is worth quoting at length a text that stresses the severity of punishment imposed on those negligent towards this hazard:

> Be particularly vigilant in the matter of fire. If there is a festival in the temple, keep close watch over the fire. At nightfall, thoroughly extinguish whatever of it remains on the hearth. In the event that there is any flame in isolated spots and also dry wood, and the person responsible for extinguishing it becomes criminally negligent in the temple, he who is guilty of the crime will perish together with his descendants – even if only the temple is destroyed and Hattusa and the king's property are not harmed. Of those who are in the temple (and thereby share in the crime of negligence), not one is to be spared; together with their descendants they shall perish. In your own interests, then, be particularly vigilant in the matter of fire.[13]

To avoid such occurrences, the *Hazannu* must have constantly been monitoring that fire safety was being maintained by citizens. Working beneath the *Hazannu* were two superintendents known as *Maškim*. One was stationed in the Upper City, the other in the Lower City. As providing alerts and guarding the city were part of the *Hazannu's* responsibilities, a herald and sentries were also included among his staff. The *Hazannu* was also responsible for securing the gates of the city each evening. Once closed, the doors were stamped with an official seal. Any tampering with the gates would be evident the next morning.

District governors (*Bel Madgalti*) were appointed in the provinces of the Hittite homeland. The governor functioned as a stand-in for the king's presence in that territory. He was required to carry out any of the monarch's orders and report back to the capital on the happenings in the region (often in person). Responsibilities included the administration of justice in the region, the upkeep of local temples, overseeing agricultural production and monitoring hostile military forces. Beyond these regions were the vassal states, where local leaders remained in power under an oath of loyalty to the Hittite king. Treaties ensured that vassals would send regular tribute and provide military assistance when necessary and forbade them from taking independent actions with other foreign powers. The status of a vassal ruler is made apparent in one such contractual agreement between the Hittite king Mursili II and his subordinate Tuppi-Teshub of Amurru:

> And as I took care of you according to the request of your father, and installed you in place of your father, I have now made you swear an oath to the king of Hatti and the land of Hatti, and to my sons and grandsons. Observe the oath and the authority of the King. I, My Majesty, will protect you, Tuppi-Teshub. And when you take a wife and produce a son, he shall later be king in the land of Amurru. As you protect My Majesty, I will likewise protect your son . . . The tribute which was imposed upon your grandfather and upon your father shall be imposed upon you: They paid 300 shekels of refined gold by the weights of Hatti, first-class and good. You shall pay it likewise. You shall not turn your eyes to another.[14]

Hittite diplomats and other officials were dispatched to these vassal states, where they worked collaboratively with the ruler of the region. However, not all subjugated territories were treated as vassals. Following Suppiluliuma I's conquest of Syria, Hittite control of this unique prize was maintained by the appointment of Hittite princes as viceroys at Carchemish and Aleppo.

### The Hittite understanding of gender and the woman's experience

Hittite society assigned traditional roles to men and women. In the myth of Appu, the protagonist reproaches his wife: 'You are a woman and think like one. You know nothing at all.'[15] Sexism permeated the ancient world, and the Hittites were no exception. Despite such societal perceptions of being the lesser gender, the female principle was still very much revered in Hittite religion, as shown by its many goddesses. Gary Beckman notes, 'In Hatti the fertility of the earth was represented by the female Sun-goddess, while the hypermasculine Storm-god stood for the fructifying water of rainfall . . . Goddesses were responsible for the thriving of grain, for the successful birth of humans, and for a myriad of other essential phenomena.'[16] Both divine and mortal women had their role to play.

A conventional construct of gender was epitomized in the symbols used to represent masculinity and femininity. The bow and arrow are the Hittite symbols of the male, while the distaff and spindle are the symbols of the female. Part of the oath of a Hittite soldier included a curse to prevent disloyalty, threatening treacherous individuals with the prospect of femininity. The masculine symbols are exchanged for feminine ones:

> He who transgresses these oaths and takes part in evil against the king, queen, and princes, may these oath deities make that man into a woman. May they make his troops women. Let them put a scarf on them. Let them break the bows, arrows, and weapons in their hands and let them place the distaff and spindle in their hands instead.[17]

Following the humiliation of being paraded around in women's attire, a disloyal soldier may then have been executed. This makes for an interesting comparison with a ritual for curing impotence, where the reverse occurs. The feminine objects are held by the man and natural order is restored by exchanging them for the male symbols:

> I place a spindle and a distaff in the patient's hand, and he comes under the gates. When he steps forward through the gates, I take the spindle and distaff away from him. I give him a bow and arrows, and say to him all the while: 'I have just taken the femininity away from you and given you masculinity in return. You have cast off the sexual behaviour expected of women; you have taken to yourself the behaviour expected of man.'[18]

In both the soldier's oath and the ritual for curing impotence, spindle and distaff are perceived as negative and inferior to the male attributes. Interestingly, for a woman who was deemed to have fertility issues, the problem was not that she had inadvertently adopted masculine characteristics. She was not made to exchange weaponry for spinning equipment. The comparison instead was to livestock, for in the ritual to bring fecundity to a woman, she was made to grasp the horn of a fertile cow, so that her house may be as fruitful as the cattle pen.[19]

The Hittite laws shine light on the woman's experience of marriage. Trevor Bryce points out: 'There is no specific word for "marry" in the Hittite language – a new husband is said to "take" his wife, and henceforth to "possess" her. Romantic love has little if any part in such a context.'[20] There are only a few references to love between partners in Hittite texts, notably that shared between power couple Puduhepa and Hattusili III. Betrothal was instigated with the *kusata* (bride price), a gift given to the prospective bride or her family by a suitor. The woman would then be given her dowry, this being her share of her family's estate. It would remain her own property, with the husband acting as its overseer. A husband would only acquire this asset in the event of being predeceased by his wife. The woman generally went to live with her husband's household. Sometimes the family of a bride might instead choose to adopt her husband (an *antiyant* marriage), in which case he would join her family's household. Both wife and husband were entitled to a request for divorce. Incest was forbidden, and adultery could result in the death penalty. If a husband caught his unfaithful spouse in bed with another and appealed to the court to spare his wife, he was also required to spare the life of her lover.

The legal clause concerning rape states: 'If a man seizes a woman in the mountains and rapes her, the man is guilty and shall die, but if he seizes her in her house, the woman is guilty and shall die. If the woman's husband catches them in the act and kills them, he has committed no offence.'[21] What is being implied here, is that if a woman was sexually attacked in a place where no one could hear her cries for help (the mountains), she was

Small silver Hittite figurine in the form of a seated woman, 14th–13th century BC.

considered innocent. In a place where she could have alerted others but neglects to (the house), the sex becomes a consensual act. The same logic is found in Deuteronomy 22:23–7. Levirate marriage is prescribed in the laws, whereby a man should marry his brother's wife in the event of his death. This was a safeguard that ensured a woman would continue to be supported following her husband's death.

Childbearing was very much an expectation for Hittite women. A woman who hoped to become pregnant might choose to sleep in a temple, anticipating that the residing deity might visit her during the night and cause her to conceive. Conception was connected with the Moon and the lunar deity Arma – the Hittite verb used to describe becoming pregnant is *armai-*, which literally means 'to be in a lunar way'.[22] Hattusili III wrote to Ramesses II requesting the assistance of an Egyptian doctor to help his mature-aged sister, Matanazi, to conceive. She had been used for a marriage alliance with the vassal ruler of the Seha River Land and an heir was needed to guarantee stability in the region. Hattusili received a blunt reply from the pharaoh: 'Look, I know about Matanazi, your sister . . . The word is that she's fifty, if not sixty years old! No one can prepare medicines to enable a fifty- or sixty-year-old woman to have children!'[23] Though a great king, Hattusili clearly did not understand menopause.

Once pregnant, a community festival was held that honoured the mother goddesses and celebrated the woman's condition. Throughout a woman's pregnancy, offerings and purifications occurred. There were prohibitions on certain foods, such as crushed cress, and on sex for a pregnant woman. She was required to eat separately from her husband, and utensils were not to be shared between them. This was to prevent the spread of pollution. The father was not present at the birth. Midwives prepared the equipment, chiefly the birthing stool, and recited incantations throughout the process. Priests also attended. In a Kizzuwatnean ritual designed to keep negative forces at bay during parturition, a priest 'smears the birthstool and the pegs with the blood of two birds, each separately. And he twice makes meat offerings of two sheep and four birds before the birthstool.'[24] The delivery usually occurred in the home. The newborn was then ceremoniously named by its father, while he dandled the infant on his knee. After a period of isolation, the mother and child were then reintegrated into the community with festivity.

Among the variety of roles they played in society, the most prominent position held by a woman was the office of queenship: the *Tawananna*. We have already met some formidable royal females. Puduhepa excelled in managing political affairs both in Hatti and with foreign powers. The sickness that plagued Hattusili III throughout his life gave the queen an opportunity to demonstrate her strong political and business acumen. After his death, she continued to play an important role at court and acted as regent for her son, Tudḫaliya IV. Conversely, we encountered the powerful Babylonian Tawananna, who was accused of abusing her power by Mursili II. Her stepson portrayed her as an extravagant individual, who introduced vulgar foreign customs to Hattusa and killed his wife through witchcraft. She was punished with ostracism. This was the fate of several other influential women at court. Hattusili I banished his own daughter and his sister, who was memorably described by the king as a snake with the vocals of oxen. We must remember that these damning portrayals reach us via reports composed by men who felt threatened by these ambitious royal women.

A queen was the high priestess of the gods. She was an active participant in religious ceremonies, and also managed the assets of temples. This role had her travel outside of the capital, on pilgrimage to important religious centres and to carry out duties at festivals that occurred all over the empire. One interesting ritual required the queen to perform a dance while holding an axe before the goddess Ishtar of Tamininga.[25] Queens would likely have been left largely responsible for the running of the capital during the frequent absences of the king on military campaigns. Just like the king, a queen continued to receive reverence after death in the royal funerary cult. Bearing children was also an important duty of the king's wife. The princesses born of the monarch became important diplomatic commodities. These women (often nameless in texts) were shipped off to foreign kings or vassals to consolidate alliances through marriage. Hittite princes were rarely used for marriage alliances, an exceptional example being the son of Suppiluliuma I who was murdered en route to marry Tutankhamun's widow. While the majority of Hittite citizens practised monogamy, the king had secondary wives and concubines for the purpose of maximizing a steady flow of child production.

Outside of the royal household, women of more humble means operated largely in domestic roles. Women could hire themselves out for work at a reduced rate. Common jobs performed by female workers included agricultural labourers, cooks, weavers, musicians, dancers and inn keepers. But even the everyday unnamed woman proved herself adaptable, as society in the capital would be dependent on the ability of a female workforce when the majority of the men were away on regular military campaigns.

Women were particularly influential in religious life. The attendants of goddesses were generally women, although priestesses could also be in the service of male deities. More than half of the authors of ritual texts were women. These were the female ritual practitioners known as ḫašauwa, the 'Wise Women'.[26] The term literally translates as 'she of birth', probably a reflection of the fact that the title was originally used for a midwife. After all, a Hittite midwife was responsible for both physically assisting a birth and reciting incantations to protect and grant longevity to a newborn. It was believed that the words of a midwife had particular sway over the gods. Great importance was attributed to human articulation in ritual. The spoken word had magical ability, exemplified in a Hittite proverb that states 'the tongue is a bridge'.[27] Effective recitation during ritual was thus a key responsibility of the ḫašauwa. The rituals conducted by the ḫašauwa relied on analogic magic, combining verbal incantation with actions performed on representative figurines and other implements. While largely concerned with healing the physical or spiritual ailments of individuals, the ḫašauwa also performed roles in the rites of state festivals. These women were literate and appear to have been multilingual, as some of their rituals of foreign origin featured spoken sections in other languages, such as Babylonian and Hurrian. Slaves could be trained in the ritual practice, as was the case for a certain *ḫašauwa* named Anniwiyani. The names of some of these wise women survive in the rituals they wrote down and performed: Alli, Tunnawiya, Paškuwatti, Mallidunna and Maštigga to pay homage to a few.[28] As with scribes, this highly skilled profession was likely inherited and passed down through generations of women.

## Slavery

The lowest class of Hittite society were the slaves. The slave was a valuable commodity (costing 20 to 30 shekels based on their level of skills) that could be bought and sold. The majority of slaves were foreign prisoners of war, who were brought back as the spoils of Hittite conquests. A person could also become enslaved as punishment for committing a serious crime, such as homicide – or the criminal may be required to give one of his sons as a slave to the victim's family. Failure to pay off a debt may also result in enslavement to the unpaid party. Slaves could, however, own property and amass enough capital to eventually buy their freedom. Used largely for agricultural labour, some slaves were given tracts of land to cultivate for themselves in addition to the work they performed on their masters' acreage. Trevor Bryce comments: 'This "enlightened" approach to slavery (as far as any slave-owning society can be called enlightened) was almost certainly pragmatically based – on the principle that the best way of maximizing human productivity is through an appropriate system of rewards and incentives.'[29] The Hittite laws indicate that slaves could accumulate such a substantial amount of wealth that it was desirable for free-born citizens to enter into marriage with them. A male slave could offer a bride price for the hand of a free-born woman. Her social status was guaranteed, and she would remain free in such a marriage. Any children born of their union would also be free. Thereby, a slave could secure freedom for his descendants.

Penalties in the laws are based on a culprit's social status, with slaves typically paying half the rate of compensation as the free-born. Clause 105 of the Laws states, 'If anyone sets fire to a field, and the fire catches a fruit-bearing vineyard, if a vine, an apple tree, a pear tree or a plum tree burns, he shall pay 6 shekels of silver for each tree. He shall replant the planting. And he shall look to his house for it. If it is a slave, he shall pay 3 shekels of silver for each tree.'[30] However, slaves are prescribed with much harsher physical punishments in the Laws. A slave who angered his master could be blinded, or have his ears and nose chopped off. One of the laws declares that 'a slave who rebels against his owner will be stuffed in a jug'.[31] While, in theory, a master had absolute power over his slaves, he was unlikely to inflict such bodily harm on these assets lightly. Mutilations would impair work capacity, and their stigma would reduce the resale value of the slave.

# EIGHT

# BEYOND THE BRONZE AGE: A CONTINUING HITTITE LEGACY

The fall of the Hittite Empire at the start of the twelfth century BC did not see a complete end to Hittite culture in the ancient Near East. Until about 700 BC, several kingdoms ruled in Anatolia and Syria that have become known as the Neo-Hittite or Syro-Hittite states. These Neo-Hittite kingdoms lacked any central authority, and competing interests often resulted in skirmishes between them. While Hittite language written in cuneiform had stopped being used, the Neo-Hittites continued to utilize the other script of Luwian hieroglyphs in rock relief. Likewise, aspects of Hittite art, architecture and religion found continuity and imitation in these Iron Age states. Tapping into the collective memory of an illustrious past provided a means for projecting authority in the time of uncertainty and change that followed the Bronze Age collapse.[1] Though traditions continued, they show increased innovation over time. The Storm-god remained a major deity for the Neo-Hittites. Their rulers sometimes adopted the names of bygone Hittite kings, including Labarna, Hattusili, Tudahaliya, Suppiluliuma and Muwatalli. They proclaimed themselves as 'Great King' in the tradition of the Bronze Age. It may even be that the remnants of the Hittite court fled to this region when Hattusa was abandoned.

A lack of Neo-Hittite records means very little is known about the formation of the kingdoms. There is, however, a wealth

Hittite motifs and Luwian hieroglyphic script found continuation in the reliefs of the Neo-Hittite period. In this example from Aslantepe, the Storm-god is depicted in both the centre and on the left, in his bull-drawn chariot. A king named as Sulumeli pours a libation before him. Behind, a servant brings forth a sacrificial bull.

of visual material, with an increase in Hittite-style public sculpture produced during this period. Lions continued to function as city gateway guardians. In the ninth century BC, at Tell Halaf, the Hittite portal sphinx was adapted with novelty into a monumental set of winged scorpion men. The entry facade of the Western Palace at this site featured three columns sculptured in the long-established form of gods standing atop their prerogative animals. In Neo-Hittite art, new scenes were blended with traditional motifs; the attributes and garb (including the iconic curled-toe boot) worn by figures persisted. Imagery of the hunt and of royalty paying homage to the divine remained popular, carved in low relief onto cliff sides and basalt panels. Such images would influence the palatial orthostats of the Neo-Assyrians. The documentation of the Neo-Assyrian Empire, which, ultimately, conquered the

Heirlooms of an empire: some of the Hittite amulets discovered in a grave from the 7th century BC at Carchemish.

Neo-Hittites, provides a major (albeit biased) source of historical information about the kingdoms.

Carchemish was the largest of the Neo-Hittite kingdoms, formerly a viceregal seat of the empire. The first Neo-Hittite ruler of Carchemish was Kuzi-Teshub. He was the son of Talmi-Teshub, the last viceroy during the Hittite period. His lineage made him a descendant of the great Hittite king Suppiluliuma I, who had first installed his son Piyassili to rule the region. Other dynasties soon supplanted this old line: the House of Suhi, followed by the House of Astiruwa. The patron deity of Carchemish and its kings was the Hittite goddess Kubaba. Neo-Hittite reliefs depict her wearing a cylindrical headdress, with a pomegranate in one hand and a mirror in the other. Carchemish was finally overthrown by the Neo-Assyrian Empire at end of the eighth century BC. The royal family and inhabitants of Carchemish were deported to Assyria before the city was repopulated with Assyrian settlers. This method of subjugation for conquered areas was standard Assyrian practice and ultimately wiped away the Neo-Hittite presence from the Near East.

The excavation of a grave at Carchemish that dates to the seventh century BC has yielded an assemblage of 29 tiny figures made of steatite, lapis lazuli and gold, now in the British Museum. The trinkets depict the Hittite gods bearing their characteristic weaponry and other implements, including the celestial winged disc. What makes these amulets particularly interesting is that they were produced much earlier than the burial itself, dating stylistically to the thirteenth century BC. The archaeologist Sir Leonard Woolley, who excavated Carchemish, wrote, 'These little figures are the jeweller's reproduction in miniature of the great rock-cut reliefs of Yazılıkaya . . . They are not copied from the Yazılıkaya reliefs but, I would suggest, they and the reliefs alike are versions of a religious and artistic theme.'[2] These 'heirloom' amulets, manufactured in the Hittite Empire, came to be preserved, handed down and then eventually deposited as grave goods during the Neo-Hittite period. Just how this occurred is a mystery. Were they perhaps carried from Hattusa at the time of its abandonment, thereafter becoming hallowed treasures of a former age?

## The place of the Hittites in modern Turkey

The rediscovery of Hittite and Neo-Hittite monuments has kindled another legacy, with these ancient peoples being regarded as a source of national pride by many modern Turks. Echoes from the Bronze Age past also resonate in Turkey's modern history. Much like the Hittite king Hattusili, who changed his name to reflect that he was the 'Man of Hattusa', in 1934 Mustafa Kemal was bestowed with the surname Atatürk that designated him as the 'Father of the Turks'. Both recognized an individual's name as a potent force for forging a new identity. And indeed, the Hittites were to play a key role in Atatürk's propaganda campaign of Turkish nationalism.

Atatürk toured archaeological sites and promoted excavations undertaken during the 1930s, taking particular interest in Turkey's Bronze Age contributions to world history. His regime saw the creation of a collective memory in which the Hittites were used to define Turkishness. The contribution of the Ottomans and Islamic identity were underplayed in favour of the Hittites, who were claimed as the original Turks. This assertion provided a unifying force for Turkey's ethnically diverse population. Many businesses and institutions founded in this era opted for Hittite names, such as Etibank ('Hittite bank'). Some Turkish citizens did likewise in 1934, when it became mandatory to adopt a hereditary family surname. More recent was the 1961 founding of Eti, producers of the packaged cakes, biscuits and chocolates ubiquitous in Turkey's roadside petrol station stores today. The snack food company named after the Hittites has a stylized Bronze Age sun disc as its logo.

The 1930s also saw development of the Sun Language Hypothesis in Turkey. This pseudoscientific linguistic theory claimed that all human languages descended from a single proto-Turkic language. In the lead up to the Second World War, when theories of racial superiority saw the emergence of eugenic policies that excluded certain ethnic groups in Europe, the Turks were taking the other extreme. They showed their superiority by making everyone Turkish. The theory conveniently allowed for the existence of foreign words in Turkish, given all were apparently derived

A replica of the Egyptian–Hittite peace treaty was gifted by the Turkish government to the United Nations in 1970.

from a common Turkic root language. It asserted the Sumerians and Hittites as the first Turks, who formed the foundations for all civilization. The basis for the Sun Language Hypothesis was that language was born from the ritual blabbering of early humans which accompanied worshipping the Sun. The discovery of the pre-Hittite bronze sun discs from Alaca Höyük fed the theory. The anthropologist Afet Inan spoke at the Second Turkish Historical Congress in 1937:

The Turkish race discovered its culture in such a place that there the sun was the most productive. The Turks who had to leave their first home chose their primary routes of migration by following the guidance of the sun. And our ancestors the Hittites, the first to establish the culture of our own home Anatolia, made a symbol of the sun. They made it the subject of the intricacy of their arts . . . These sun disks, decorated with various geometrical designs, will take an important position in our history as the symbol of Turkish thought and art.[3]

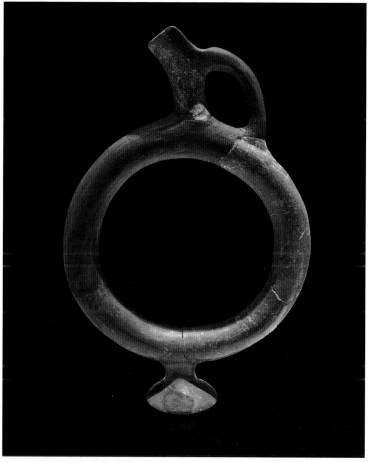

Wine blessed by the sun? A selling point for souvenir jugs based off this reconstructed Hittite ring-shaped vessel from the 16th century BC.

Turkey's early responses to the Hittites showcase how the past can be reshaped for an agenda and loaded with political meaning. A more subtle example persists today. Visitors to Cappadocia's many pottery shops are likely to receive a sales pitch about a so-called Hittite wine jug. The ceramic in question bares the pleasing form of a footed vessel with a doughnut-shaped body. It rises into an upward-angled spout and has a small handle on its neck. Charismatic pottery salesmen delight tourists by narrating that the Hittites apparently held such vessels up to the Sun. Shining through the hole in the centre of the jug, the Sun thus bestowed a solar blessing upon the contents. While a sixteenth-century BC terracotta vessel of this ringed form was excavated at Hattusa, there is no references to such a practice in Hittite literature. Another version holds that the wine pourer would thread his arm through the centre and rest the jug on his shoulder. The Hittites offer a good opportunity to sell a product with some modern mythologizing. The example from Hattusa is of plain, fired red clay, not glazed and elaborately coloured as in the 'reproductions' it has inspired. The unique Bronze Age ceramic form is often applied with designs resembling Ottoman *iznik* tiles, a blend of different cultures from Turkey's rich past. Such fusion of different traditions would probably be very appealing to the Hittites!

It is these qualities of adoption and adaption that make their unique history so appealing. Today Hittite civilization is often lost in popular representations of the ancient world. While Pharaoh Ramesses the Great is a household name, his contemporaries Mutawalli and Hattusili are not. The Hittites seldom make an appearance in books, films and television shows of the trendy historical-fiction genre. No shortage of drama is found in the documents that have shaped our understanding of their history, both inscribed on clay cuneiform tablets and carved in hiero-glyphs upon stone monuments. Despite the millennia between us, the voices of these first known Indo-European speakers still have the ability to fascinate and move us. Their unique con-glomerate society featured distinctive traits, from fighting with cheese to a legal system that emphasized compensation. The surviving objects they produced include small stone seals that marked identity and silver cups in the form of animals. Allusions to their culture were preserved in ancient Greek religion and in the Bible. The lacunae in Hittite texts and awaited discoveries only incite the imagination to fill the many gaps that remain.

## 1 Rediscovering a Lost Civilization

1 J. D. Hawkins, 'Tarkasnawa King of Mira "Tarkondemos", Boğazköy Sealings and Karabel', *Anatolian Studies*, XLVIII (1998), pp. 1–31.
2 Georges Perrot was the first to correctly identify Hattusa as the capital in 1886.
3 Trevor Bryce, *Warriors of Anatolia* (London and New York, 2019), p. 14.
4 Ibid., p. 75.
5 J. D. Hawkins and A. Davies, 'On the Problems of Karatepe: The Hieroglyphic Text', *Anatolian Studies*, XXVIII (1978), pp. 103–19.
6 Note that it was also written in cuneiform. Luwian language cuneiform tablets have been excavated at Hattusa.
7 Annick Payne, 'Writing Systems and Identity', in *Anatolian Interfaces: Hittites, Greeks and Their Neighbours*, ed. B. J. Collins, M. R. Bachvarova and I. Rutherford (Oxford, 2008), pp. 117–22.

## 2 Political and Military History

1 Billie Jean Collins, *The Hittites and Their World* (Atlanta, GA, 2007), p. 29.
2 Trevor Bryce, *The Kingdom of the Hittites* (Oxford, 2005), p. 19.
3 Ibid., p. 64.
4 Trevor Bryce, *Life and Society in the Hittite World* (Oxford, 2002), p. 230.
5 Trevor Bryce, *Warriors of Anatolia* (London and New York, 2019), p. 35.
6 Ibid., p. 36.
7 Ibid., p. 37.
8 Ibid., p. 39.
9 Ibid., p. 71.
10 Ibid., p. 76.
11 Collins, *The Hittites and Their World*, p. 45.
12 William L. Moran, *The Amarna Letters* (Baltimore, MD, 1992), EA 27, p. 89.
13 Itamar Singer and Harry A. Hoffner, *Hittite Prayers* (Atlanta, GA, 2002), Catalogue of Hittite Texts (CTH), 378.I, pp. 63–4.

14  Ibid., CTH 378.IV, p. 65.
15  Ibid., CTH 378.III, p. 57.
16  Ibid., CTH 70, p. 76.
17  Ibid., CTH 380, pp. 72–3.
18  Bryce, *Life and Society in the Hittite World*, p. 181.
19  The Ramesseum and the Precinct of Amun-Re at the Temple of Karnak.
20  Collins, *The Hittites and Their World*, p. 56.
21  Bryce, *The Kingdom of the Hittites*, pp. 28–78.
22  Michael Moore, 'Hittite Queenship: Women and Power in Hittite Anatolia', PhD thesis, University of California, Los Angeles, 2018, p. 130.
23  Collins, *The Hittites and Their World*, p. 68.
24  Bryce, *Warriors of Anatolia*, p. 234.
25  Ibid., pp. 256–7.
26  Ibid., p. 262.
27  Eric H. Cline, *1177 BC: The Year Civilization Collapsed* (Princeton, NJ, 2014), p. 165.

## 3 Via Diplomacy or War: Hittite International Relations

1  Trevor Bryce, *The Kingdom of the Hittites* (Oxford, 2005), p. 258.
2  William L. Moran, *The Amarna Letters* (Baltimore, MD, 1992), EA 44, p. 117.
3  Ibid., EA 161, pp. 247–8.
4  Ibid., EA 51, p. 122.
5  Ibid., EA 166 and 167, pp. 254–5.
6  Billie Jean Collins, *The Hittites and Their World* (Atlanta, GA, 2007), p. 48.
7  Ibid., p. 49.
8  Gary M. Beckman and Harry A. Hoffner, *Hittite Diplomatic Texts* (Atlanta, GA, 1996), p. 149.
9  Trevor Bryce, *Letters of the Great Kings of the Ancient Near East* (London and New York, 2003), p. 110.
10  Trevor Bryce, *Life and Society in the Hittite World* (Oxford, 2002), pp. 99–100.
11  Collins, *The Hittites and Their World*, p. 108.
12  Gary M. Beckman, 'Blood in Hittite Ritual', *Journal of Cuneiform Studies*, LXIII (2011), p. 95.
13  Bryce, *Life and Society in the Hittite World*, p. 99.
14  Collins, *The Hittites and Their World*, p. 110.

## 4 Major Sites of the Hittites

1  Trevor Bryce, *Life and Society in the Hittite World* (Oxford, 2002), p. 251.
2  Although a number of scholars attribute the Südburg structure to Šuppiluliuma I, rather than II, there is no definite proof one way or the other.

3 E. Zangger and R. Gautschy, 'Celestial Aspects of Hittite Religion: An Investigation of the Rock Sanctuary Yazılıkaya', *Journal of Skyscape Archaeology*, v/1 (2019), pp. 5–38.

4 Billie Jean Collins, *The Hittites and Their World* (Atlanta, GA, 2007), p. 192.

5 Yiğit Erbil and Alice Mouton, 'Water in Ancient Anatolian Religions: An Archaeological and Philological Inquiry on the Hittite Evidence', *Journal of Near Eastern Studies*, LXXI/1 (2012), p. 74.

6 Ibid., p. 71. I have substituted the term 'Dark Earth' in their translation to 'Netherworld'.

7 Ahmet Ünal, 'The Textual Illustration of the "Jester Scene" on the Sculptures of Alaca Höyük', *Anatolian Studies*, XLIV/4 (1994), pp. 207–18.

## 5 ART AND MATERIAL CULTURE

1 Billie Jean Collins, *The Hittites and Their World* (Atlanta, GA, 2007), p. 17.

2 Billie Jean Collins, 'Animals in the Religions in the Ancient World', in *A History of the Animal World in the Ancient Near East*, ed. B. J. Collins (Leiden, 2002), p. 316.

3 While ritual texts provide much written evidence for animal sacrifice, there is little visual representation. A rare example is the relief referred to here from Alaca Höyük.

4 Gary M. Beckman and Harry A. Hoffner, *Hittite Diplomatic Texts* (Atlanta, GA, 1996), p. 19.

5 Collins, *The Hittites and Their World*, p. 39.

6 Harry A. Hoffner, *Hittite Myths* (Atlanta, GA, 1998), p. 69.

7 Gary M. Beckman, 'Proverbs and Proverbial Allusions in Hittite', *Journal of Near Eastern Studies*, XLV/1 (1986), p. 22.

8 Collins, 'Animals in the Religions in the Ancient World', p. 314.

9 Hoffner, *Hittite Myths*, pp. 18–19.

10 Ibid., p. 54.

11 Billie Jean Collins, 'Ḫattušili I, the Lion King', *Journal of Cuneiform Studies*, L (1998), p. 19.

12 Ibid., p. 16.

13 Y. Heffron, 'The Material Culture of Hittite "God-Drinking"', *Journal of Ancient Near Eastern Religions*, XIV/2 (2014), p. 169.

14 Harry A. Hoffner, 'Oil in Hittite Texts', *Biblical Archaeologist*, LVIII/2 (1995), p. 112.

## 6 HITTITE RELIGION AND MYTHOLOGY

1 Michael B. Hundley, 'The God Collectors: Hittite Conceptions of the Divine', *Altorientalische Forschungen*, XLI/2 (2014), pp. 176–200.

2 Harry A. Hoffner, *Hittite Myths* (Atlanta, GA, 1998), p. 43.

3 James B. Pritchard, *Ancient Near Eastern Texts Relating to the Old Testament with Supplement* (Princeton, NJ, 1969), p. 121.

4 Hoffner, *Hittite Myths*, p. 50.

5 Ibid., pp. 15, 21.
6 The Storm-god at Liḫzina, CTH 331.1.
7 Hoffner, *Hittite Myths*, p. 81.
8 Ibid., p. 83.
9 Gary M. Beckman, *The Hittite Gilgamesh* (Atlanta, GA, 2019), p. 5.
10 Billie Jean Collins, 'Divine Wrath and Divine Mercy of the Hittite and Hurrian Deities', in *Divine Wrath and Divine Mercy in the World of Antiquity*, ed. Reinhard Gregor Katz and Hermann Spieckermann (Tübingen, 2008), pp. 67–77 (pp. 74–5).
11 Billie Jean Collins, 'Ritual Meals in the Hittite Cult', in *Ancient Magic and Ritual Power*, ed. Marvin Meyer and Paul Mirecki (Leiden, 2015), pp. 77–92 (p. 77).
12 Itamar Singer and Harry A. Hoffner, *Hittite Prayers* (Atlanta, GA, 2002), p. 63.
13 Ibid., p. 35.
14 Alfonso Archi, 'The Anatolian Fate-Goddesses and Their Different Traditions', in *Diversity and Standardization: Perspectives on Ancient Near Eastern Cultural History*, ed. Eva Cancik-Kirschbaum et al. (Berlin and Boston, MA, 2013), pp. 1–26 (p. 1).
15 Ibid., p. 6.
16 Ibid., p. 7.
17 Ibid., p. 15.
18 Theo P. J. van den Hout, 'Death as Privilege: The Hittite Royal Funerary Ritual', in *Hidden Futures: Death and Immortality in Ancient Egypt, Anatolia, the Classical, Biblical and Arabic-Islamic World*, ed. J. M. Bremer, Theo P. J. van den Hout and R. Peters (Amsterdam, 1994), pp. 37–76 (p. 40).
19 Archi, 'The Anatolian Fate-Goddesses and Their Different Traditions', p. 11.
20 Alfonso Archi, 'The Soul Has to Leave the Land of the Living', *Journal of Ancient Near Eastern Religions*, VII/2 (2007), p. 173.
21 Ibid., p. 190.
22 Singer and Hoffner, *Hittite Prayers*, p. 38.
23 Archi, 'The Soul Has to Leave the Land of the Living', p. 189.
24 Van den Hout, 'Death as Privilege', p. 59.
25 Ibid., p. 69.
26 Ibid., p. 46.
27 Gary M. Beckman, 'Bilingual Edict of Ḫattušili I', in *The Context of Scripture*, vol. II: *Monumental Inscriptions from the Biblical World* (Leiden, 2002), pp. 79–81.
28 Alice Mouton, 'Animal Sacrifice in Hittite Anatolia', in *Animal Sacrifice in the Ancient Greek World*, ed. Sarah Hitch and Ian Rutherford (Cambridge, 2017), p. 249.
29 Gary M. Beckman, 'Blood in Hittite Ritual', *Journal of Cuneiform Studies*, LXIII (2011), p. 101.
30 Singer and Hoffner, *Hittite Prayers*, p. 51.

31  Francesco G. Barsacchi, 'Distribution and Consumption of Food in Hittite Festivals', in *Economy of Religions in Anatolia: From the Early Second to the Middle of the First Millennium BCE*, proceedings of an international conference (Bonn, 2018), p. 7.

32  Billie Jean Collins, 'Animals in the Religions in the Ancient World', in *A History of the Animal World in the Ancient Near East*, ed. B. J. Collins (Leiden, 2002), p. 329.

33  Ibid., p. 100.

34  Billie Jean Collins, 'Women in Hittite Religion', in *Women in Antiquity: Real Women Across the Ancient World* (Abingdon and New York, 2016), p. 332.

35  Xen. Const. Lac. 2.9, available at www.perseus.tufts.edu, accessed 19 July 2022.

36  Michele Cammarosano, *Hittite Local Cults* (Atlanta, GA, 2018), p. 129.

37  Stefano de Martino, 'Music, Dance, and Processions in Hittite Anatolia', in *Civilizations of the Ancient Near East*, ed. J. Sasson (New York, 1995), vol. IV, p. 2668.

38  Trevor Bryce, *Life and Society in the Hittite World* (Oxford, 2002), p. 191.

39  Procedure of the KIN Oracles and quote adapted from Billie Jean Collins, *The Hittites and Their World* (Atlanta, GA, 2007), pp. 167–8.

40  Singer and Hoffner, *Hittite Prayers*, p. 32.

41  Gary M. Beckman, 'On Hittite Dreams', in *Ipamati kistamati pari tumatimis: Luwian and Hittite Studies,* presented to J. David Hawkins on the occasion of his seventieth birthday, ed. I. Singer (Tel Aviv, 2010), p. 30.

42  Alice Mouton, 'Portent Dreams in Hittite Anatolia', in *Perchance to Dream: Dream Divination in the Bible and the Ancient Near East* (Atlanta, GA, 2018), p. 35.

43  Beckman, 'On Hittite Dreams', p. 28.

44  Ibid.

45  Gary M. Beckman, 'From Cradle to Grave: Women's Role in Hittite Medicine and Magic', *Journal of Ancient Civilizations*, VIII (1993), p. 30.

46  Collins, *The Hittites and Their World*, p. 180.

47  Alice Mouton, '"Dead of Night" in Anatolia: Hittite Night Rituals', *Religion Compass*, II/1 (2008), p. 8.

48  Billie Jean Collins, 'The Puppy in Hittite Ritual', *Journal of Cuneiform Studies*, XLII/2 (1990), pp. 211–26.

49  Ibid.

50  Bryce, *Life and Society in the Hittite World*, p. 155.

51  Albrecht Goertz, 'Hittite Myths, Epics and Legends', in *Ancient Near Eastern Texts relating to the Old Testament*, 3rd edn (Princeton, NJ, 1969), p. 207.

52  Collins, *The Hittites and Their World*, p. 185.

53  Ibid., p. 188.

7 SOCIETY AND THE LAW

1  Harry A. Hoffner, *The Laws of The Hittites: A Critical Edition* (Leiden, 1997), p. 23.

2 Trevor Bryce, *Life and Society in the Hittite World* (Oxford, 2002), p. 39.

3 Harry A. Hoffner, 'Daily Life Among the Hittites', in *Life and Culture in the Ancient Near East*, ed. R. Averbeck et al. (Bethesda, MD, 2003), pp. 95–120 (pp. 109–8).

4 Ronald L. Gorny, 'Viniculture and Ancient Anatolia', in *The Origins and Ancient History of Wine*, ed. Patrick E. McGovern, Stuart J. Fleming and Solomon H. Katz (Amsterdam, 1996), pp. 133–75 (p. 153).

5 Ibid., p. 164.

6 Harry A. Hoffner, 'Oil in Hittite Texts', *Biblical Archaeologist*, LVIII/2 (1995), p. 110.

7 Ibid., p. 109.

8 Ibid.

9 Ibid., p. 112.

10 Hoffner, 'Daily Life Among the Hittites', p. 102.

11 Billie Jean Collins, *The Hittites and Their World* (Atlanta, GA, 2007), p. 93.

12 Ibid., p. 92.

13 Bryce, *Life and Society in the Hittite World*, p. 253.

14 Collins, *The Hittites and Their World*, pp. 106–7.

15 Gary M. Beckman, 'The Old Woman: Female Wisdom as a Resource and a Threat in Hittite Anatolia', in *Audias fabulas veteres: Anatolian Studies in Honor of Jana Součková-Siegelová* (Leiden, 2016), p. 48.

16 Ibid., p. 50.

17 Collins, *The Hittites and Their World*, p. 182.

18 Bryce, *Life and Society in the Hittite World*, p. 166.

19 Ibid.

20 Trevor Bryce, 'The Role and Status of Women in Hittite Society', in *Women in Antiquity: Real Women across the Ancient World*, ed. S. L. Budin and J. M. Turfa (London and New York, 2016), p. 310.

21 Ibid., p. 314.

22 Gary M. Beckman, 'Birth and Motherhood among the Hittites', in *Women in Antiquity: Real Women across the Ancient World*, ed. Budin and Turfa, p. 322.

23 Bryce, *Life and Society in the Hittite World*, p. 171.

24 Collins, *The Hittites and Their World*, p. 180.

25 Billie Jean Collins, 'Women in Hittite Religion', in *Women in Antiquity: Real Women across the Ancient World*, ed. Budin and Turfa, p. 331.

26 Beckman, 'The Old Woman', p. 48.

27 Gary M. Beckman, 'Proverbs and Proverbial Allusions in Hittite', *Journal of Near Eastern Studies*, XLV/1 (1986), p. 25.

28 Beckman, 'The Old Woman', p. 55.

29 Bryce, *Life and Society in the Hittite World*, p. 78.

30 Collins, *The Hittites and Their World*, p. 123.

31 Ibid., p. 135.

## 8 Beyond the Bronze Age: A Continuing Hittite Legacy

1 Virginia R. Herrmann and Giuliana Paradiso, 'Are Monuments History? (Neo-) Hittite Meditations on Two Memes', *The Ancient Near East Today*, VIII/8 (August 2020), www.asor.org.

2 Charles Leonard Woolley and Richard D. Barnett, *Carchemish: Report on the Excavations at Jerablus on Behalf of the British Museum* (London, 1952), pp. 255–7.

3 Wendy M. K. Shaw, 'Whose Hittites, and Why? Language, Archaeology and the Quest for the Original Turks', in *Archaeology Under Dictatorship*, ed. M. L. Galaty and C. Watkinson (New York, 2004), p. 147.

Archi, A., 'The Soul Has to Leave the Land of the Living', *Journal of Ancient Near Eastern Religions*, VII/2 (2007), pp. 169–95

—, 'The Anatolian Fate-Goddesses and their Different Traditions', in *Diversity and Standardization – Perspectives on Ancient Near Eastern Cultural History*, ed. E. Cancik-Kirschbaum, J. Klinger and G.G.W. Müller (Berlin, 2013), pp. 1–26

Barsacchi, Francesco G., 'Distribution and Consumption of Food in Hittite Festivals', *Economy of Religions in Anatolia: From the Early Second to the Middle of the First Millennium BCE*, proceedings of an international conference (Bonn, 2018), pp. 5–20

Beckman, Gary M., 'Proverbs and Proverbial Allusions in Hittite', *Journal of Near Eastern Studies*, XLV/1 (1986), pp. 19–30

—, 'From Cradle to Grave: Women's Role in Hittite Medicine and Magic', *Journal of Ancient Civilizations*, VIII (1993), pp. 25–39

—, 'Bilingual Edict of Ḫattušili I', in *The Context of Scripture*, vol. II: *Monumental Inscriptions from the Biblical World*, ed. W. W. Hallo and K. L. Younger Jr (Leiden, 2002), pp. 79–81

—, 'On Hittite Dreams', in *Ipamati kistamati pari tumatimis: Luwian and Hittite Studies,* presented to J. David Hawkins on the occasion of his seventieth birthday, ed. I. Singer (Tel Aviv, 2010), pp. 26–31

—, 'Blood in Hittite Ritual', *Journal of Cuneiform Studies*, LXIII (2011), pp. 95–102

—, 'Birth and Motherhood among the Hittites', in *Women in Antiquity: Real Women across the Ancient World*, ed. S. L. Budin and J. M. Turfa (London and New York, 2016), pp. 319–28

—, 'The Old Woman: Female Wisdom as a Resource and a Threat in Hittite Anatolia', in *Audias fabulas veteres: Anatolian Studies in Honor of Jana Součková-Siegelová*, ed. Š. Velhartická (Leiden, 2016), pp. 48–57

—, *The Hittite Gilgamesh* (Atlanta, GA, 2019)

—, and Harry A. Hoffner, *Hittite Diplomatic Texts* (Atlanta, GA, 1996)

Bryce, Trevor, *Life and Society in the Hittite World* (Oxford, 2002)

—, *Letters of the Great Kings of the Ancient Near East* (London and New York, 2003)

—, *The Kingdom of the Hittites* (Oxford, 2005)

—, *The World of the Neo-Hittite Kingdoms: A Political and Military History* (Oxford, 2012)

—, 'The Role and Status of Women in Hittite Society', in *Women in Antiquity: Real Women across the Ancient World*, ed. S. L. Budin and J. M. Turfa (London and New York, 2016), pp. 303–18

—, *Warriors of Anatolia: A Concise History of the Hittites* (London and New York, 2019)

Cammarosano, Michele, *Hittite Local Cults* (Atlanta, GA, 2018)

Cline, Eric H., *1177 BC: The Year Civilization Collapsed* (Princeton, NJ, 2014)

Collins, Billie Jean, 'The Puppy in Hittite Ritual', *Journal of Cuneiform Studies*, XLII/2 (1990), pp. 211–26

—, 'Ḫattušili I, the Lion King', *Journal of Cuneiform Studies*, L (1998), pp. 15–20

—, 'Animals in the Religions in the Ancient World', in *A History of the Animal World in the Ancient Near East*, ed. B. J. Collins (Leiden, 2002), pp. 309–34

—, *The Hittites and Their World* (Atlanta, GA, 2007)

—, 'Divine Wrath and Divine Mercy of the Hittite and Hurrian Deities', in *Divine Wrath and Divine Mercy in the World of Antiquity*, ed. R. G. Kratz and H. Spieckermann (Tübingen, 2008), pp. 67–77

—, 'Ritual Meals in the Hittite Cult', in *Ancient Magic and Ritual Power*, ed. P. Mirecki and M. Meyer (Leiden, 2015), pp. 77–92

—, 'Women in Hittite Religion', in *Women in Antiquity: Real Women across the Ancient World,* ed. S. L. Budin and J. M. Turfa (London and New York, 2016), pp. 329–41

De Martino, Stefano, 'Music, Dance, and Processions in Hittite Anatolia', in *Civilizations of the Ancient Near East*, ed. J. M. Sasson (New York, 1995), vol. IV, pp. 2661–9

Erbil, Yiğit, and Alice Mouton, 'Water in Ancient Anatolian Religions: An Archaeological and Philological Inquiry on the Hittite Evidence', *Journal of Near Eastern Studies*, LXXI/1 (2012), pp. 53–74

Gorny, Ronald L., 'Viniculture and Ancient Anatolia', in *The Origins and Ancient History of Wine*, ed. P. E. McGowern, S. J. Fleming and S. H. Katz (Amsterdam, 1996), pp. 133–74

Hawkins, J. D., 'Tarkasnawa King of Mira "Tarkondemos", Boğazköy Sealings and Karabel', *Anatolian Studies*, XLVIII (1998), pp. 1–31

—, and A. Davies, 'On the Problems of Karatepe: The Hieroglyphic Text', *Anatolian Studies*, XLVIII (1978), pp. 103–19

Heffron, Y., 'The Material Culture of Hittite "God-Drinking"', *Journal of Ancient Near Eastern Religions*, XIV/2 (2014), pp. 164–85

Hoffner, Harry A., 'Oil in Hittite Texts', *Biblical Archaeologist*, LVIII/2 (1995), pp. 108–14

—, *Hittite Myths* (Atlanta, GA, 1998)

—, 'Daily Life Among the Hittites', in *Life and Culture in the Ancient Near East*, ed. R. E. Averbeck, M. W. Chavalas and D. B. Weisberg (Bethesda, MD, 2003), pp. 95–118

Hundley, Michael B., *Gods in Dwellings: Temples and Divine Presence in the Ancient Near East* (Atlanta, GA, 2013)

—, 'The God Collectors: Hittite Conceptions of the Divine', *Altorientalische Forschungen*, XLI/2 (2014), pp. 176–200

Mellaart, James, 'The Late Bronze Age Monuments of Eflatun Pınar and Fasıllar Near Beyşehir', *Anatolian Studies*, XII (1962), pp. 111–17

Moore, M., 'Hittite Queenship: Women and Power in Hittite Anatolia', PhD thesis, University of California, Los Angeles, 2018

Moran, William L., *The Amarna Letters* (Baltimore, MD, 1992)

Mouton, Alice, '"Dead of Night" in Anatolia: Hittite Night Rituals', *Religion Compass*, II/1 (2008), pp. 1–17

—, 'Animal Sacrifice in Hittite Anatolia', in *Animal Sacrifice in the Ancient Greek World*, ed. S. Hitch and I. Rutherford (Cambridge, 2017), pp. 239–52

—, 'Portent Dreams in Hittite Anatolia', in *Perchance to Dream: Dream Divination in the Bible and the Ancient Near East*, ed. E. J. Hamori and J. Stökl (Atlanta, 2018), pp. 27–41

—, and Yiğit Erbil, 'Dressing Up for the Gods: Ceremonial Garments in Hittite Cultic Festivals according to the Philological and Archaeological Evidence', *Journal of Ancient Near Eastern Religions*, XX/1 (2020), pp. 48–86

Payne, Annick, 'Writing Systems and Identity', in *Anatolian Interfaces: Hittites, Greeks and Their Neighbors*, ed. B. J. Collins, M. R. Bachvarova and I. Rutherford (Oxford, 2008), pp. 117–22

Pritchard, James B., *Ancient Near Eastern Texts Relating to the Old Testament with Supplement* (Princeton, NJ, 1969)

Rutherford, Ian, *Hittite Texts and Greek Religion: Contact, Interaction, and Comparison* (Oxford, 2020)

Shaw, Wendy M. K., 'Whose Hittites, and Why? Language, Archaeology and the Quest for the Original Turks', in *Archaeology Under Dictatorship*, ed. M. L. Galaty and C. Watkinson (New York, 2004), pp. 131–53

Singer, Itamar, and Harry A. Hoffner, *Hittite Prayers* (Atlanta, GA, 2002)

Taracha, Piotr, 'The Sculptures of Alacahöyük: A Key to Religious Symbolism in Hittite Representational Art', *Near Eastern Archaeology*, LXXV/2 (2012), pp. 108–15

Ünal, Ahmet, 'The Textual Illustration of the "Jester Scene" on the Sculptures of Alaca Höyük', *Anatolian Studies*, XLIV/4 (1994), pp. 207–18

Van den Hout, Theo P. J., 'Death as Privilege. The Hittite Royal Funerary Ritual', in *Hidden Futures: Death and Immortality in Ancient Egypt, Anatolia, the Classical, Biblical and Arabic-Islamic World*, ed. Th. P. J. van den Hout and R. Peters (Amsterdam, 1994), pp. 37–75

Woolley, Charles Leonard, and Richard David Barnett, *Carchemish: Report on the Excavations at Jerablus on Behalf of the British Museum* (London, 1952)

Zangger, E., and R. Gautschy, 'Celestial Aspects of Hittite Religion: An Investigation of the Rock Sanctuary Yazılıkaya', *Journal of Skyscape Archaeology*, V/1 (2019), pp. 5–38

In addition to the above books and articles there is a fantastic online resource called Hittite Monuments, run by Tayfun Bilgin. It provides visual reference material for all major Hittite and Neo-Hittite archaeological sites. A virtual map allows visitors of the website to explore the various locations where remnants of Hittite culture have been discovered. It can be accessed at www.hittitemonuments.com.

# ACKNOWLEDGEMENTS

Gratitude is owed to all my friends and family who listened, advised and pointed me towards sources of information as I worked on this book. Thank you for showing interest, checking in on my progress and forgiving my absences when I was lost in the Bronze Age.

A big thank you is due to my guinea pigs, Geoffrey Page and Wendy Stone, who read the earliest drafts. Candace Richards has been most enthusiastic about my ideas and encouraged me to speak on Queen Puduhepa at the conference 'Modern Women of the Past? Unearthing Gender and Antiquity' in March 2021. I want to thank Michael Leaman and everyone at Reaktion Books for their patience, understanding and backing of this project. I would like to also acknowledge the debt I owe to the great scholars of Hittitology whose many writings I sifted through, especially the works of Trevor Bryce, Billie Jean Collins, Gary Beckman and Harry A. Hoffner.

Recognition is due to my colleagues in the Collection Management Team at the Chau Chak Wing Museum who have been supportive of this side project and always showed interest while I prattled at morning tea about life in the Hittite world – Maree Clutterbuck, Christopher Jones, Rachel Lawrence, Virginia Ho, Madeleine Snedden, Julie Taylor, Aggie Lu, David James, Matthew Huan, Silvia Da Rocha, Emma Conroy and Katt Johns.

Thank you also to you, the reader. I hope the Hittite world intrigues and entertains you. May you one day visit Turkey and venture into the land of Hatti yourself.

# PHOTO ACKNOWLEDGEMENTS

The author and publishers wish to express their thanks to the below sources of illustrative material and/or permission to reproduce it. Some locations of artworks are also given below, in the interest of brevity:

akg-images: p. 78 (Gerard DeGeorge); Alamy: pp. 75, 92, 105, 158, 163 (all: funkyfood London – Paul Williams); © The Trustees of the British Museum, London: pp. 100, 159; courtesy of Tayfun Bilgin @ www.hittitemonuments.com: pp. 48, 119; Getty Images: p. 93 (DEA/ARA GULKER); The Metropolitan Museum of Art, New York: pp. 28 (Rogers Fund, 1967/Accession Number: 67.182.1), 88 left and right (Gift of Nanette B. Kelekian, in memory of Charles Dikran and Beatrice Kelekian, 1999/Accession Number: 1999.325.203), 98 (Rogers Fund, 1967/Accession Number: 67.182.2), 99 (Gift of Norbert Schimmel Trust, 1989/ Accession Number: 1989.281.12), 109 (Gift of Norbert Schimmel Trust, 1989/ Accession Number: 1989.281.10), 110 (Gift of Norbert Schimmel Trust, 1989/ Accession Number: 1989.281.11), 111 (Gift of Norbert Schimmel Trust, 1989/ Accession Number: 1989.281.10), 151 (Gift of Norbert Schimmel Trust, 1989/ Accession Number: 1989.281.17); Museum of Fine Arts, Boston: pp. 89 (Frank B. Bemis Fund/Accession Number: 1977.114), 112 (Gift of Landon T. and Lavinia Clay in honor of Malcolm Rogers/Accession Number: 2004.2230); Oriental Institute, The University of Chicago: p. 81 (Registration Number: A22292); The Walters Arts Museum, Baltimore, Maryland: pp. 14 (CC0/Accession Number: 57.2058), 21 (CC0/Accession Number: 57.1512); United Nations Photo: p. 162 (Teddy Shen).

Félix Marie Charles Texier (Public Domain), the copyright holder of the image on p. 19, is published online under conditions imposed by a Creative Commons Attribution-Share Alike 3.0 Unported License. (Author: Near_East_topographic_map-blank.svg: Sémhur/Derivative work: Ikonact.) Klaus-Peter Simon, the copyright holder of the images on pp. 20, 82, 95 top and centre, 96, 102 and 103; Iocanus (talk), the copyright holder of the image on p. 44; Olaf Tausch, the copyright holder of the image on p. 45; Ingeborg Simon, the copyright

*181*

Page numbers in *italics* refer to illustrations